Power Maths

Year 4 Practice Book

What did you learn last term in maths?

Draw or write one thing you remember.

This book belongs to _____ .

My class is _____ .

Contents

This looks like a good challenge!

It is time to do some practice!

How to use this book

Do you remember how to use this **Practice Book**?

Use the **Textbook** first to learn how to solve this type of problem.

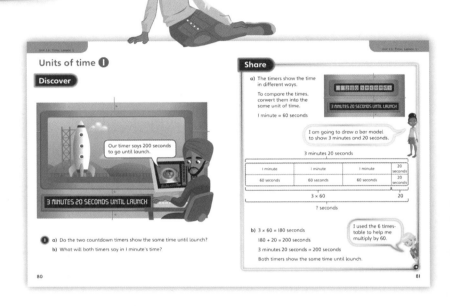

This shows you which **Textbook** page you need.

Have a go at questions by yourself using this **Practice Book**. Use what you have learnt.

Challenge questions make you think hard!

Questions with this light bulb make you think differently.

Reflect

Each lesson ends with a **Reflect** question so you can think about what you have learnt.

Use **My power points** at the back of this book to keep track of what you have learnt.

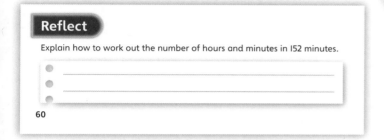

Reflect

Explain how to work out the number of hours and minutes in 152 minutes.

60

My journal

At the end of a unit your teacher will ask you to fill in **My journal**.

This will help you show how much you can do now that you have finished the unit.

→ Textbook 4C p100   Unit 13: Time

End of unit check

My journal

1. How long have you been alive? Is this more, equal to or less than 100 months?

Use this space to show your working.

I know I have been alive more / the same as / less than 100 months because _____

Keywords:
convert, months, years, units

Power check

How do you feel about your work in this unit?   😕?   🙂   😊

73

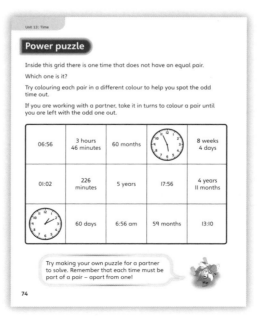

Unit 13: Time

Power puzzle

Inside this grid there is one time that does not have an equal pair.

Which one is it?

Try colouring each pair in a different colour to help you spot the odd time out.

If you are working with a partner, take it in turns to colour a pair until you are left with the odd one out.

06:56	3 hours 46 minutes	60 months	(clock)	8 weeks 4 days
01:02	226 minutes	5 years	17:56	4 years 11 months
(clock)	60 days	6:56 am	59 months	13:10

Try making your own puzzle for a partner to solve. Remember that each time must be part of a pair – apart from one!

74

→ **Textbook 4C p8**

Making a whole

1 Use the hundredths grids to find the missing digits and complete the statements.

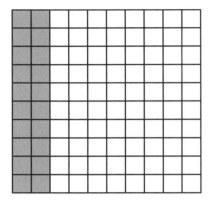

a) $0.\boxed{} + 0.\boxed{} = 1$

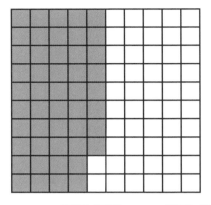

c) $0.\boxed{}\boxed{} + 0.\boxed{}\boxed{} = 1$

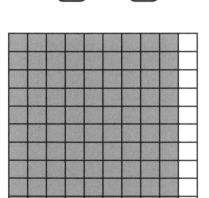

b) $0.\boxed{} + 0.\boxed{} = 1$

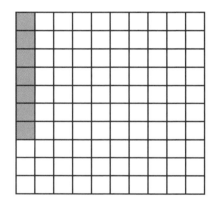

d) $0.\boxed{}\boxed{} + 0.\boxed{}\boxed{} = 1$

2 Work out the missing numbers in the bar models.

a)

1	
$0.\boxed{}\boxed{}$	0.39

b)

1	
0.13	$0.\boxed{}\boxed{}$

3 Draw the correct counters to complete the part-whole models.
Then complete the matching statements.

a) 0.☐ + ☐.☐ = 1

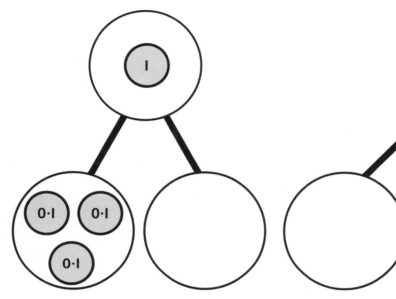

c) ☐.☐ + 0·2 + ☐.☐ = 1

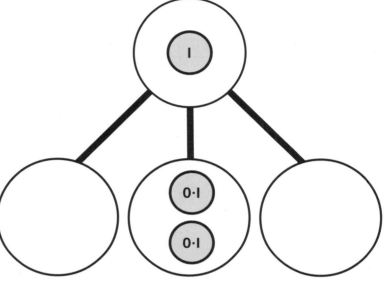

b) 0·1 + ☐.☐ + 0·4 = 1

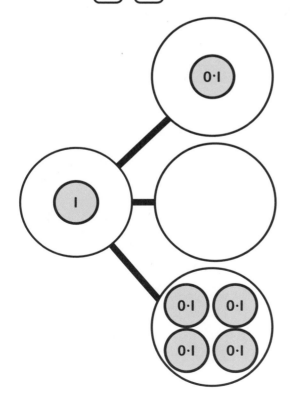

I wonder if there is more than one way to do this one.

7

4 Complete the calculations.

a) $0.6 + \boxed{} = 1$

c) $0.32 + \boxed{} = 1$

b) $1 = \boxed{} + 0.84$

d) $\boxed{} + 0.09 = 1$

5 Complete the missing digits to make the calculations correct.

a) $0.\boxed{}3 + 0.7\boxed{} = 1$

c) $1 - 0.6\boxed{} = 0.3\boxed{}$

b) $1 = 0.1\boxed{} + 0.\boxed{}9$

d) $0.\boxed{}6 = 1 - 0.\boxed{}4$

6 Use the number cards so that each row and column adds up to 1 whole.

CHALLENGE

a)

| 0.3 | 0.5 | 0.6 | 0.1 | 0.2 |

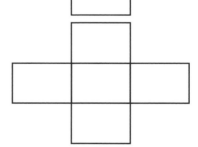

b)

| 0.32 | 0.23 | 0.2 | 0.29 | 0.48 |

Reflect

Use a ten frame and ten 0.1 counters to write as many different calculations as you can that make 1 whole. How do your number bonds to 10 help you?

Writing decimals

1 What numbers are shown on the place value grids?

a)

T	O	•	Tth	Hth
	1 1 1 1 1 1	•	0·1 0·1 0·1 0·1 0·1 0·1 0·1 0·1	

[ ] . [ ]

b)

T	O	•	Tth	Hth
	1 1 1 1 1 1 1	•		0·01 0·01 0·01 0·01 0·01 0·01 0·01 0·01 0·01

[ ] . [ ]

c)

T	O	•	Tth	Hth
10		•	0·1 0·1 0·1 0·1 0·1	

[ ]

d)

T	O	•	Tth	Hth
		•		0·01 0·01 0·01 0·01

[ ]

2 Complete the bar model and the calculation.

3·49	
3	0·09

$3·49 = 3$ _____ $+$ [ ] tenths $+ 9$ _____

9

3 Which image does not represent 0·12?

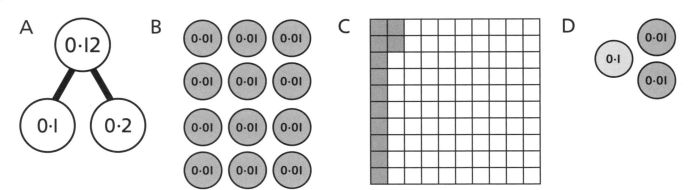

Image _____ does not represent 0·12.

4 Complete the table.

a)	7 ones + 2 tenths + I hundredth	7·▢▢
b)	2 tens + 9 _____ + 3 tenths + 4 _____	▢9·▢4
c)	▢ hundred + ▢ ones + ▢ _____	I▢5·6
d)	I ten + 7 ones + I hundredth	▢▢·▢▢
e)	5 tenths + 3 hundredths	▢·▢▢
f)	53 hundredths	▢·▢▢

What do you notice about e) and f)? Why is this?

_____

_____

5 Mo, Emma and Danny are playing a number game. Each child gives one clue. Draw lines to show which number matches each child.

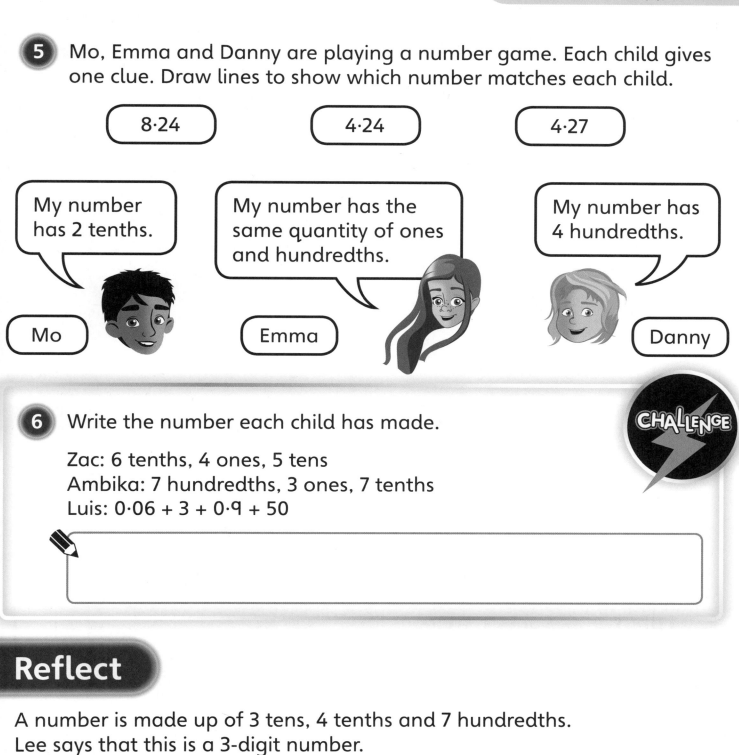

8·24   4·24   4·27

My number has 2 tenths.

My number has the same quantity of ones and hundredths.

My number has 4 hundredths.

Mo   Emma   Danny

6 Write the number each child has made.

CHALLENGE

Zac: 6 tenths, 4 ones, 5 tens
Ambika: 7 hundredths, 3 ones, 7 tenths
Luis: 0·06 + 3 + 0·9 + 50

Reflect

A number is made up of 3 tens, 4 tenths and 7 hundredths.
Lee says that this is a 3-digit number.
Is Lee correct? Explain your answer.

→ Textbook 4C p16

Comparing decimals

1 Which number is larger? Circle the larger number on the left. Then write the signs in the circles on the right to make the statements correct.

a) 9·5 or 9·9

9·5 ◯ 9·9

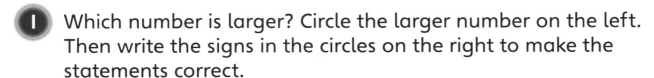

O	•	Tth
1 1 1 1 1 1 1 1 1	•	0·1 0·1 0·1 0·1 0·1

O	•	Tth
1 1 1 1 1 1 1 1 1	•	0·1 0·1 0·1 0·1 0·1 0·1 0·1 0·1 0·1

b) 8·13 or 8·31

8·13 ◯ 8·31

O	•	Tth	Hth
1 1 1 1 1 1 1 1	•	0·1	0·01 0·01 0·01

O	•	Tth	Hth
1 1 1 1 1 1 1 1	•	0·1 0·1 0·1	0·01

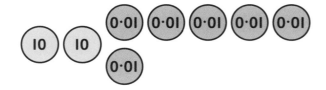

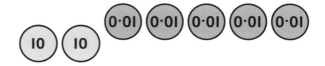

c) 20·06 or 20·05

20·06 ◯ 20·05

d) 100·25 or 100·52

100·25 ◯ 100·52

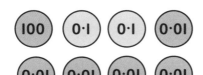

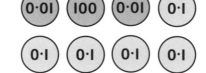

2 Richard makes two numbers.

O	•	Tth	Hth
① ① ①	•	0·1 0·1	0·01

O	•	Tth	Hth
① ① ①	•		0·01 0·01 0·01 0·01 0·01 0·01 0·01

He says that 3·21 is less than 3·07 because it uses fewer counters. Explain why Richard is not correct.

_____

_____

3 Which image shows the smaller number? Fill in the boxes.

O	•	Tth	Hth
	•	0·1 0·1 0·1	0·01 0·01

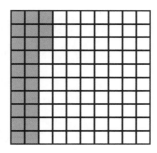

☐ ◯ ☐

4 Complete each sentence using <, > or =.

a) 4·56 ◯ 4·72

b) 12·9 ◯ 18·7

c) 9·45 ◯ 9·05

d) 3·18 ◯ 3·12

e) 26·39 ◯ 27·49

f) 120·26 ◯ 120·26

g) 3 tenths + 5 hundredths ◯ 5 tenths and 4 hundredths

5 Insert numbers to make the statements correct. Find three different answers for each question.

a) 6·74 > 6·☐4

6·74 > 6·☐4

6·74 > 6·☐4

b) 2·☐3 < 2·3☐

2·☐3 < 2·3☐

2·☐3 < 2·3☐

c) ☐9·☐5 < 1☐·☐☐

☐9·☐5 < 1☐·☐☐

☐9·☐5 < 1☐·☐☐

6 Write some numbers that are less than 30·03 but more than 2 tens, 9 ones, 9 tenths and 2 hundredths.

_____

_____

Reflect

Isla is comparing the numbers 57·89 and 57·88.

To compare the numbers, Isla should start with the _____ .

Then she should look at the _____ .

● Then _____

● _____ .

●

Ordering decimals

1 Put these numbers in order starting with the smallest.

| 7·2 | | 6·7 | | 7·9 |

O	•	Tth
7	•	2

O	•	Tth
6	•	7

O	•	Tth
7	•	9

Smallest [ ] , [ ] , [ ] Largest

2 a) Which place value grid shows the greatest number?

T	O	•	Tth	Hth
1	0	•	0	7

T	O	•	Tth	Hth
1	0	•	7	9

T	O	•	Tth	Hth
1	0	•	9	7

T	O	•	Tth	Hth
1	0	•	0	9

b) Order the numbers from largest to smallest.

[ ] > [ ] > [ ] > [ ]

3 a) Put the numbers in order starting with the smallest.

27·24   72·45   27·48   7·42

Smallest [ ] , [ ] , [ ] , [ ] Largest

b) Put the numbers in order starting with the largest.

4·53   4·59   5·94   5·49

Largest [ ] , [ ] , [ ] , [ ] Smallest

4 Which of these lists of numbers is not in ascending order?

A 0·77, 0·78, 0·87   C 3·14, 3·41, 4·13, 4·31

B 0·2, 0·3, 0·7   D 23·2, 23·1, 23·3

List _____ is not in ascending order.

5 Which child is incorrect? Explain your answer.

_____

_____

_____

_____

6 Five boys compete in a 100-metre race. The results are shown in the table.

Name	Time (in seconds)
Mo	28·02
Danny	28·42
Andy	27·79
Ebo	29·53
Lee	28·24

a) Write the times from smallest to greatest.

b) Who was the fastest?

_____ was the fastest.

I wonder if the fastest time will be the smallest or the biggest time.

c) Who was the slowest?

_____ was the slowest.

7 Put a digit in each box so the numbers are in ascending order.

CHALLENGE

4·0☐ , 4·☐9, ☐·01, ☐·☐☐ , 5·☐2

Reflect

Convince your partner that 0·62 < 0·65 < 0·71.

→ Textbook 4C p24

Rounding decimals

 a) Round 2·7 to the nearest whole number.

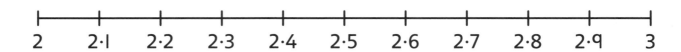

2·7 is between ☐ and ☐ .

2·7 rounded to the nearest whole number is ☐ .

b) Round 10·3 to the nearest whole number.

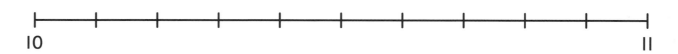

10·3 is between ☐ and ☐ .

10·3 rounded to the nearest whole number is ☐ .

c) Round 28·3 to the nearest whole number.

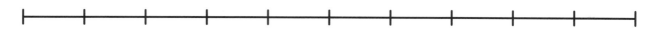

28·3 is between ☐ and ☐ .

28·3 rounded to the nearest whole number is ☐ .

2 Round these numbers to the nearest whole number.

a)

T	O	•	Tth
	⬤⬤⬤⬤⬤ ⬤⬤⬤⬤	•	⬤⬤⬤⬤⬤ ⬤

b)

T	O	•	Tth
⬤⬤		•	⬤⬤⬤⬤⬤ ⬤⬤⬤

a) ☐ rounded to the nearest whole number is ☐ .

b) ☐ rounded to the nearest whole number is ☐ .

3 Round these numbers to the nearest whole number.

a) 5·4 ☐

b) 12·9 ☐

c) 65·3 ☐

d) 0·4 ☐

e) 50·2 ☐

f) 150·2 ☐

g) 400·1 ☐

h) 89·9 ☐

4 Which of these cannot be Mo's number? Explain your answer.

55·2   54·8   54·5   55·5   55·1

> I rounded a number to the nearest whole number. The answer is 55.

Mo

_____

_____

_____

5 Complete the sentences.

a) 4·9 rounded to the nearest _____ is 5.

b) ☐·5 rounded to the nearest whole number is 9.

c) 12·☐ rounded to the nearest whole number is 12.

d) ☐☐·☐ rounded to the nearest whole number is 23.

6 Use the number cards to make as many numbers as you can with one decimal place. All your numbers must round to 80 as the nearest whole number.

CHALLENGE

| 0 | 3 | 4 |

| 5 | 7 | 8 |

Reflect

Explain how to use the tenths digit to help you round 43·6 to the nearest whole number.

Halves and quarters

1 Use the hundredths grids to help you write these decimals as fractions.

a) $0 \cdot 25 = \dfrac{\square}{\square}$

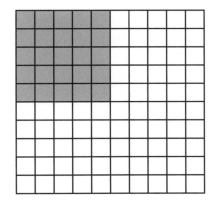

b) $0 \cdot 50 = \dfrac{\square}{\square}$

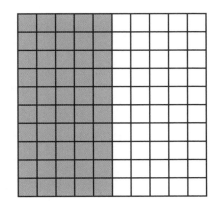

2 Alex is working out the decimal equivalent of $\frac{3}{4}$.

Her answer is $\frac{3}{4} = 3 \cdot 4$.

a) Colour the hundredths grid to show Alex is incorrect.

b) What is the correct answer?

$\frac{3}{4} = \boxed{}$

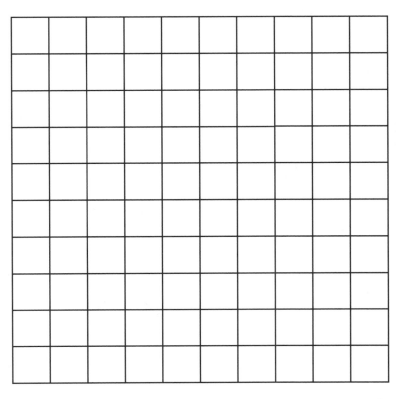

3 Use the number lines to complete the decimal equivalents.

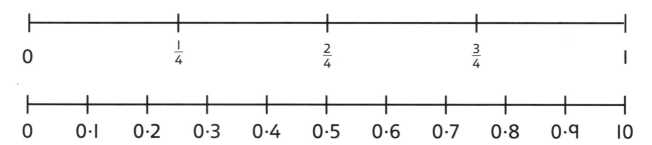

a) $\frac{1}{4} =$ [ ]

c) $\frac{3}{4} =$ [ ]

b) $\frac{2}{4} =$ [ ]

d) $\frac{1}{2} =$ [ ]

4 **a)** Colour in 0·25 of this shape.

Use your knowledge of equivalent fractions to help you colour in the shapes.

b) Colour in 0·5 of this shape.

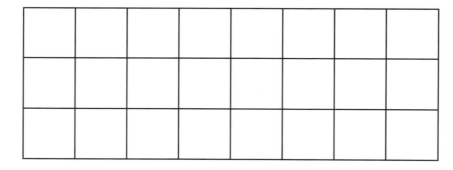

c) Colour in 0·75 of this shape.

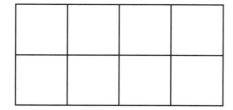

22

5 Zac has 0·5 of the apples. Emma has $\frac{1}{2}$ of the apples.

I think that Zac has 5 apples and Emma 2 apples.

Olivia

Bella

Zac and Emma have the same number of apples.

Who is correct, Olivia or Bella? Explain your answer.

_____

_____

6 Lee has some grey counters and 6 white counters.
0·25 of his counters are white.
How many of his counters are grey?

CHALLENGE

Lee has ⬚ grey counters.

Reflect

Use the hundredths grid to show that $\frac{3}{4}$ is equal to 0·75. Explain your answer below.

→ Textbook 4C p32

Problem solving – decimals

1 Complete the missing numbers.

I kg = [   ] g

3 kg = [   ] g

8,600 g = [   ] kg and [   ] g

[   ] g = 5 kg and 300 g

2 Order the weights from heaviest to lightest.

 2 kg   2 g   200 g   2 kg 200 g

_____

_____

3 Circle the correct amount that matches each picture.

a)

(I litre)

100 ml
or
1,000 ml?

b)

(1,500 ml)

15 litres
or
I l 500 ml?

c)

capacity
8 [   ]

8 litres
or
8 ml?

d)

(2 l 30 ml)

2,030 ml
or
230 ml?

4 How many of the children can go on the ride?

[ ] children are tall enough to go on the ride.

5 The length of the football field is 700 metres. The perimeter of the football field is 2 kilometres.

What is the width of the football field?

The width of the football field is [ ] metres.

6 **a)** 6,500 m = 6 km and [ ] m

b) 6,300 m = [ ] km and [ ] m

c) [ ] m = 5 km and 700 m

d) [ ] m = 3 km and 500 m

e) [ ] m = 3 km and 50 m

25

7 Complete the calculations.

a) 1 litre – 200 ml = _____

b) 50 g + ☐ g = 3 kg

c) 8 kg and 300 g + ☐ kg and ☐ g = 10 kg

8 Put these measurements in order, starting with the smallest.

CHALLENGE

450 ml, $\frac{1}{2}$ a litre, 0·25 of 4 litres, 1 l 200 ml, 102 millilitres

Can you convert all the measurements into millilitres?

Reflect

Explain how to convert litres to millilitres, or kilograms to grams, or kilometres to metres.

End of unit check

My journal

| 7·2 | 7·20 | 0·27 |

What is the same about the numbers?

_____

_____

_____

_____

What is different about the numbers?

_____

_____

_____

_____

Keywords:

tenths   hundredths   decimal digit   place value

Power check

How do you feel about your work in this unit?

Power puzzle

Work out how many litres each container can hold.

Jug = 5 × glasses

Bucket = 7 × jugs

Barrel = 20 × buckets

Glass = 200 ml

Paddling pool = 8 × barrels

Container	Number of litres the container holds
glass	
jug	
bucket	
barrel	
paddling pool	

Work out how many glasses it would take to fill up a paddling pool.

Pounds and pence

1 How much money is in each box?

Write each amount in pence. Add the 100s first.

a)
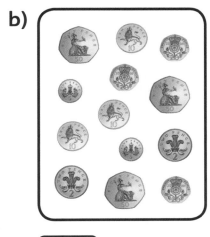

☐ pence

b)

☐ pence

c)
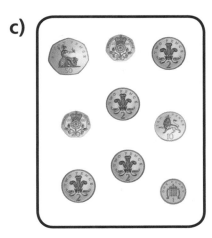

☐ pence

2 How much money is in each box?

Write each amount in pounds and pence.

a)

☐ pounds

☐ pence

b)

☐ pounds

☐ pence

c)

☐ pounds

☐ pence

3 **a)** Circle £8·72.

b) Circle £12·18.

4 Complete the part-whole models.

a)

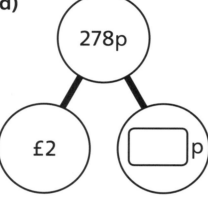

278p

£2

p

c)

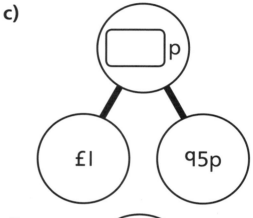

p

£1   95p

b)

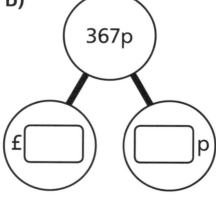

367p

£   p

d)

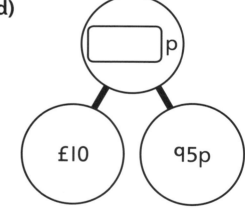

p

£10   95p

5 Write the totals in pounds and pence.

a) £1 + 50p + 20p + 20p + 5p + 2p = £ ☐ . ☐

b) £1 + £1 + £1 + 50p + 50p + 5p + 1p = £ ☐ . ☐

c) 20p + £1 + 50p + 10p + 50p + 10p = £ ☐ . ☐

6 Complete the following equivalents.

a) 258p = £ ☐

b) 370p = £ ☐

c) 408p = £ ☐

d) 1,257p = £ ☐

e) £1·18 = ☐ p

f) £8·95 = ☐ p

g) ☐ p = £2·09

h) ☐ p = £2·90

i) £11·15 = ☐ p

j) £9 = ☐ p

7 Four boxes contain different amounts of money.

CHALLENGE

- Box A contains 300p.
- Box B contains 10 times as much as Box A.
- Box C contains 10p more than Box A.
- Box D contains 100p less than Box B.

How much money is in each box?

Write your answers in pounds.

Box A = £ ☐   Box B = £ ☐   Box C = £ ☐   Box D = £ ☐

Reflect

Describe three ways you can write how much money is here in total.

_____

_____

→ Textbook 4C p44

Pounds, tenths and hundredths

1 How much money is shown?

a)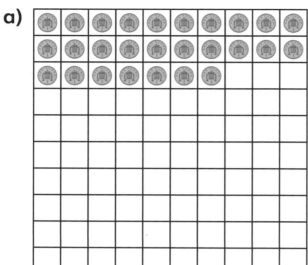

b)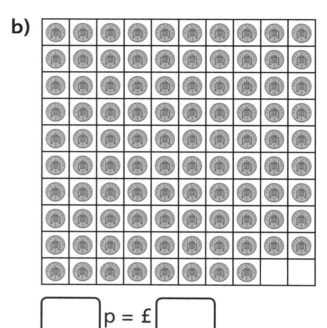

a) [　]p = £[　]

b) [　]p = £[　]

How did you work out your answer to part b)?

_____

_____

_____

2 How much money is here?

a)

[　]p = £[　]

b)

[　]p = £[　]

3 How much money is in each box?

Write your answer in pounds.

a)

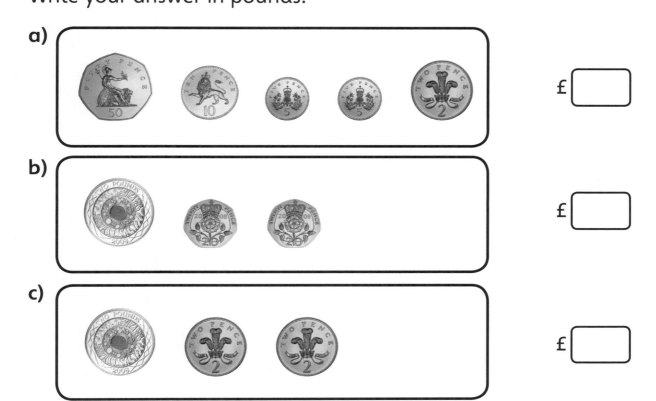

£ ⬚

b)

£ ⬚

c)

£ ⬚

4 **a)** Circle £0·27.

b) Circle £1·30.

c) Circle £1·03.

5 Aki has some money in his hand.

Aki writes this as £4·3.

Is Aki correct? If not, explain his mistake.

_____

_____

_____

_____

6 **a)** Complete the table. Write your answers in pence.

CHALLENGE

$\frac{3}{10}$ of £1	$\frac{3}{100}$ of £1	$\frac{73}{100}$ of £1	$\frac{9}{10}$ of £1	$\frac{90}{100}$ of £1
30p				

b) Amal buys a stamp. It costs him $\frac{3}{5}$ of £1.

If he pays with £1, how much change does he get?

Amal gets £ [   ] change.

Reflect

What is the same and what is different about £1·30 and £1·03?

_____

_____

_____

Ordering amounts of money

1 **a)** Circle the least expensive item.

Explain how you know.

_____

_____

b) Circle the most expensive item.

Explain how you worked this out.

_____

_____

2 Circle all the items you could buy with a £5 note.

35

3 Complete each statement with a <, >, or = sign.

a) 72p ◯ 50p   £2 ◯ £8

   72p ◯ 500p   £2 ◯ 200p

   72p ◯ 5p   £2 ◯ £2·05

   72p ◯ £5   £2 ◯ 195p

b) Seven pounds eighty pence ◯ £7·09

   £5·99 ◯ six pounds

4 Put these amounts in order from the least to the greatest.

a) £5·25   255 pence   £2·05   £0·25

_____

b) £0·84   408 pence   £8·40   4 pounds eighty pence   £8·04

_____

5 Put these amounts in order from the greatest to the least.

a) 98 pence   eight pounds ninety pence   £0·89   £0·99

_____

_____

b) 1 pound 1 pence   £0·01   11 pounds   £1·11   110 pence

_____

6 Use these digits to make the statements true.

| 5 | 6 | 8 | 9 |

a) £4·75 > £4·☐2

c) £475 > £4☐5

b) £47·50 < £4☐·50

d) £0·47 < £0·☐2

7 Use the clues to match the child to the correct money bag. **CHALLENGE**

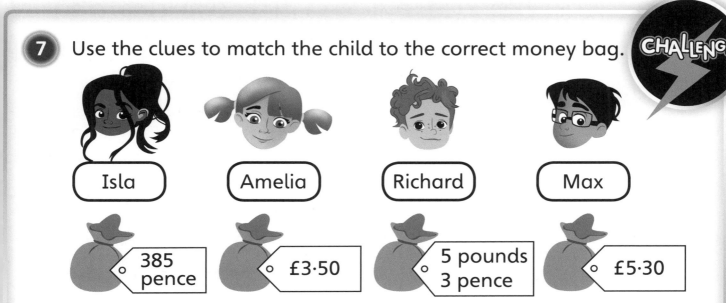

Isla   Amelia   Richard   Max

385 pence   £3·50   5 pounds 3 pence   £5·30

Clues:
- Amelia has the greatest amount of money.
- Richard and Isla have the same amount of pounds.
- Richard has more money than Isla.

Reflect

Isla says '257 pence is greater than 3 pounds as 257 > 3.'

Do you agree with Isla? Explain why or why not.

_____

_____

→ Textbook 4C p52

Rounding money

1 Round each of the following amounts to the nearest pound.

a) £1·89

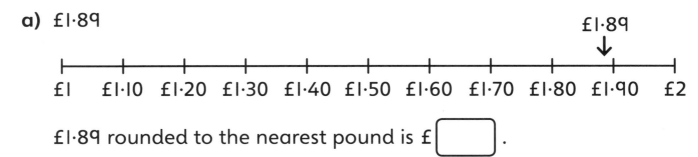

£1·89 rounded to the nearest pound is £ ☐ .

b) £3·27

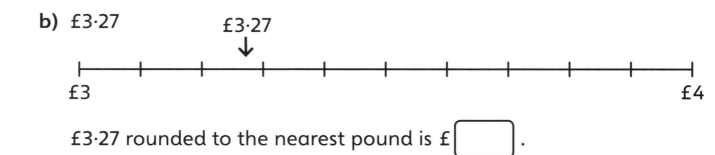

£3·27 rounded to the nearest pound is £ ☐ .

c) £9·50

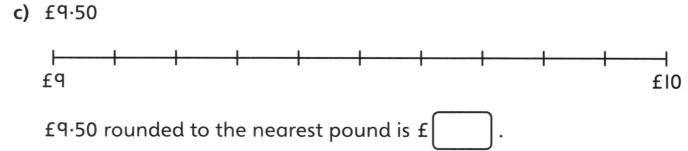

£9·50 rounded to the nearest pound is £ ☐ .

d)

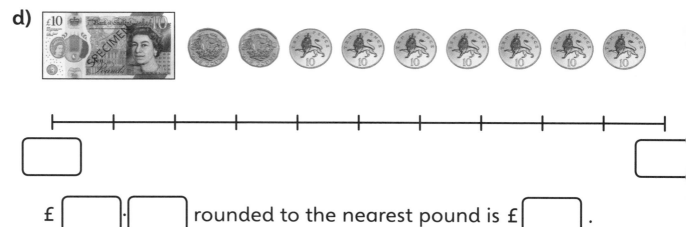

£ ☐ · ☐ rounded to the nearest pound is £ ☐ .

2 Round each of the following numbers to the nearest 10p.

a) £2·38

£2·30 ——————————————————— £2·40

£2·38 rounded to the nearest 10p is £ ☐ .

b) £0·75

£0·70 ——————————————————— £0·80

£0·75 rounded to the nearest 10p is £ ☐ .

3 Complete the table to show the rounded values.

Item	Price rounded to the nearest £1	Price rounded to the nearest 10p
£1·95		
£8·24		
£3·50		

4

| £4·95 | £5·49 | £5·92 | £4·22 | £5·50 |

Circle the items that round to £5 to the nearest £1.

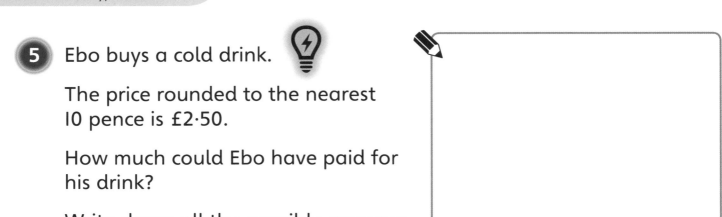

5 Ebo buys a cold drink.

The price rounded to the nearest 10 pence is £2·50.

How much could Ebo have paid for his drink?

Write down all the possible answers.

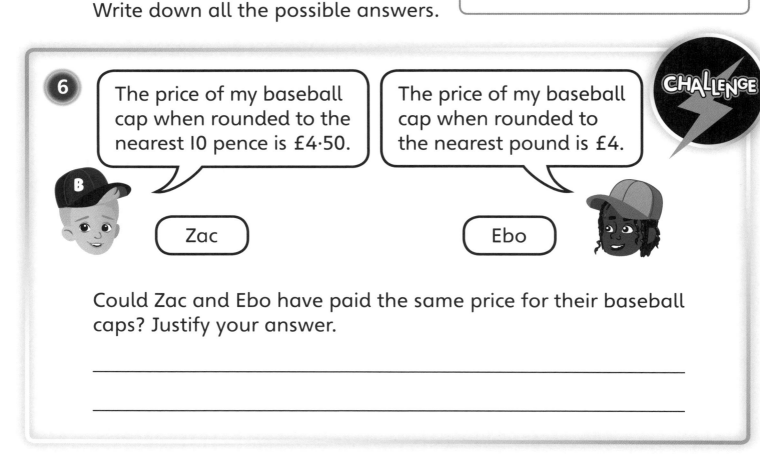

6

The price of my baseball cap when rounded to the nearest 10 pence is £4·50.

Zac

The price of my baseball cap when rounded to the nearest pound is £4.

Ebo

CHALLENGE

Could Zac and Ebo have paid the same price for their baseball caps? Justify your answer.

_____

_____

Reflect

Explain how to round £3·89 to the nearest £1 and the nearest 10p.

- _____
- _____
-

Using rounding to estimate money

1 Bella buys the following items for her dog.

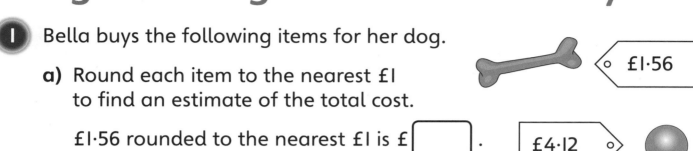

a) Round each item to the nearest £1
   to find an estimate of the total cost.

   £1·56 rounded to the nearest £1 is £ ⬚ .

   £4·12 rounded to the nearest £1 is £ ⬚ .

   £ ⬚ + ⬚ = £ ⬚

   An estimate of the total cost is £ ⬚ .

b) Round each item to the nearest 10p to find an estimate of the
   total cost.

   £1·56 rounded to the nearest 10p is £ ⬚ .

   £4·12 rounded to the nearest 10p is £ ⬚ .

   Add the pounds £ ⬚ + £ ⬚ = £ ⬚

   Add the pence ⬚ p + ⬚ p = ⬚ p

   So £ ⬚ and ⬚ p = £ ⬚

   An estimate of the total cost is £ ⬚ .

c) Which estimate is most accurate? Why?

   _____

   _____

   _____

2 Estimate the total cost by rounding each item to the nearest 10p.

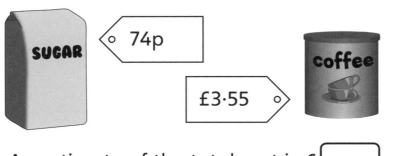

74p

£3·55

coffee

An estimate of the total cost is £ ⬚ .

3 Max buys these items.

£1·89

£0·95

£3·75

Max wants to estimate the total cost.

He rounds each number to the nearest £1.

Does Max have an over or under estimate for the total cost?

Use workings to explain your answer.

_____

_____

4 What is the greatest amount of money Holly could have in her purse?

The greatest amount of money Holly could have in her purse is £ ⬚ .

When I round the money in my purse to the nearest £1, I get £7.

Holly

5 Sofia wants to buy a car costing £7,959.

She has saved £1,875.

Estimate how much more money Sofia needs to save.

I estimate Sofia needs to save £ _____ .

6 Lexi has £20. She wants to buy some items with these costs. **CHALLENGE**

£5·43   £2·07   £6·30   £4·49   £2·26

She rounds each price to the nearest £1.
'I estimate the total to be £19, so I have enough money.'
Why might Lexi not be correct?

_____

_____

Reflect

Andy wants to work out the total cost of four objects.
He rounds each price to the nearest £1.
Write down one advantage and one disadvantage of Andy's method.

Problem solving – pounds and pence

1 **a)** How much money does Max have?

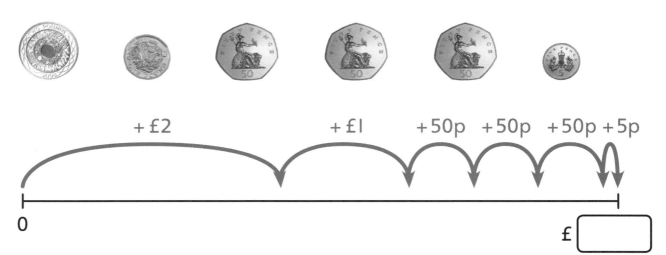

+ £2   + £1   +50p +50p   +50p +5p

0

£ ☐

b) How much money does Olivia have?

Olivia has £☐ and ☐p.

c) How much money do Max and Olivia have altogether?

Add up the pounds. £☐ + £☐ = £☐

Add up the pence. ☐p + ☐p = ☐p

£☐ and ☐p = £☐

Max and Olivia have £☐ in total.

2 Jamilla buys the following items for lunch.

How much does she spend in total?

£2·45 = £2 and ☐ p

£1·59 = £1 and ☐ p

£1·59

£2·45

3 Work out the totals.

a) £2·48 + £30·08 = ☐

b) 72p and £4·95 = ☐

4 Reena spends £2·85 on a large birthday balloon.

She pays with a £5 note.

How much change does she get from £5?

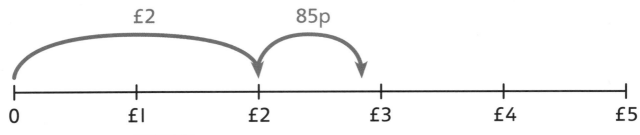

£2   85p

0   £1   £2   £3   £4   £5

Reena gets £ ☐ change.

5 Max spends £6·35. How much change would he get from a £10 note?

6 Lexi buys a DVD and a basketball using a £20 note and a £5 note.

What is the minimum number of coins she will get in her change?

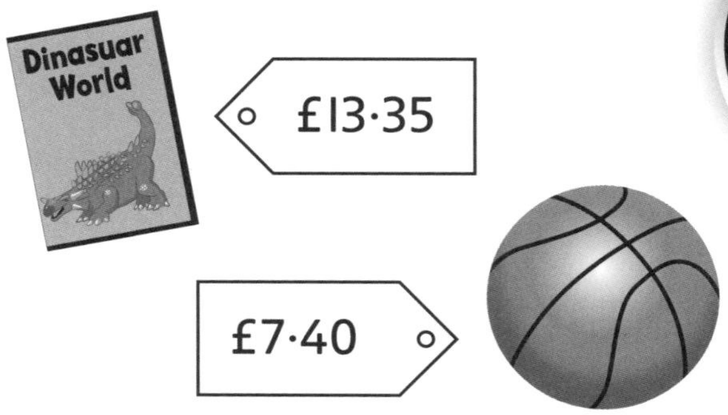

Dinasuar World

£13·35

£7·40

CHALLENGE

Reflect

Prove Richard will get some change from a £5 note if he buys 3 items costing £2·55, 70p and £1·68.

Problem solving – multiplication and division

1 A glass of milk costs £1·26.

How much do 3 glasses of milk cost?

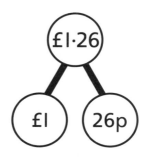

$3 \times £1 =$ ☐ $3 \times 26p =$ ☐

£ ☐ and ☐ p = £ ☐

3 glasses of milk cost £ ☐ .

2 Work out the following multiplications.

Write your answers in pounds.

a) 48p × 7

```
    4 8
×     7
_____
```

$48 \times 7 =$ ☐ p

☐ p = £ ☐

b) 5 × 92p

```
    9 2
×     5
_____
```

$5 \times 92p =$ ☐ p

☐ p = £ ☐

3 Work out the following calculations.

a) £3·18 × 6 = £ ☐

b) 5 × £7·49 = £ ☐

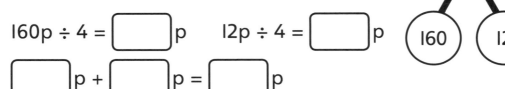

4 a) 4 scones cost 172p in total.

How much does 1 scone cost?

160p ÷ 4 = ☐ p   12p ÷ 4 = ☐ p

☐ p + ☐ p = ☐ p

A scone costs ☐ p.

172

160   12

b) 4 rulers cost £1·72 in total.

How much does 1 ruler cost?

1 ruler costs £ ☐ .

5 Work out the following divisions.

a) £2·76 ÷ 3 = ☐

b) £2·76 ÷ 2 = ☐

6 Find $\frac{2}{3}$ of £9·72.

$\frac{2}{3}$ of £9·72 = £ ☐

7 Toshi is hosting a barbeque.

He needs 12 burgers and 12 bread buns.

- Toshi knows that 3 burgers cost £4·62.

- He also knows that 5 bread buns cost £1·20.

How much does it cost him in total to buy the burgers and buns?

CHALLENGE

The total cost is £ ☐ .

Reflect

A book costs £7·99. How could you work out the cost of 8 books?
Did your partner work it out the same?

_____

_____

_____

→ **Textbook 4C p68**

Solving two-step problems

1 Work out the total cost of buying 4 lemons and 4 peppers.

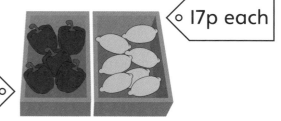

○ 17p each

23p each ○

a) Use the method of multiplying, then adding.

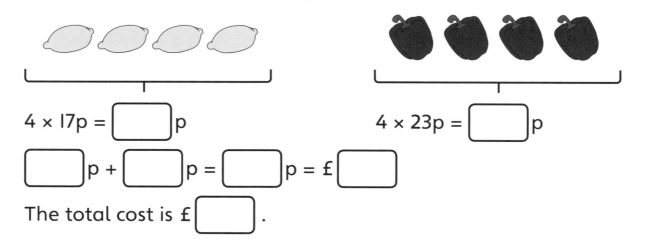

$4 \times 17p = $ ⬚ p $4 \times 23p = $ ⬚ p

⬚ p + ⬚ p = ⬚ p = £ ⬚

The total cost is £ ⬚ .

b) Use the method of adding, then multiplying.

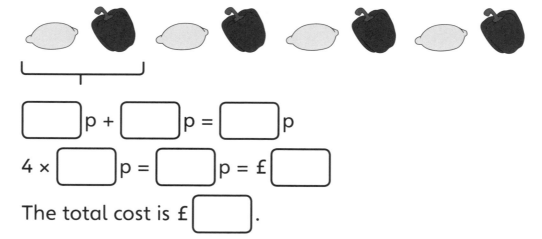

⬚ p + ⬚ p = ⬚ p

$4 \times$ ⬚ p = ⬚ p = £ ⬚

The total cost is £ ⬚ .

c) Which method did you find easier? Why?

_____

_____

2 A pack of stickers costs 80p. A pencil costs 45p.

Tom buys 3 packs of stickers and I pencil.

How much does Tom spend?

Tom spends £ [ ] .

3 There are some items for sale in a shop.

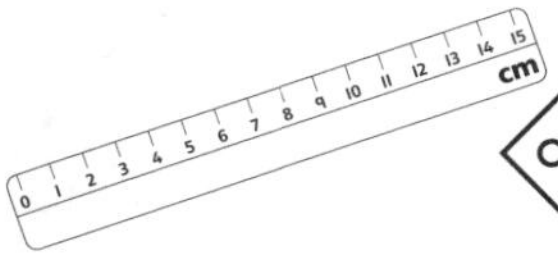

35p each 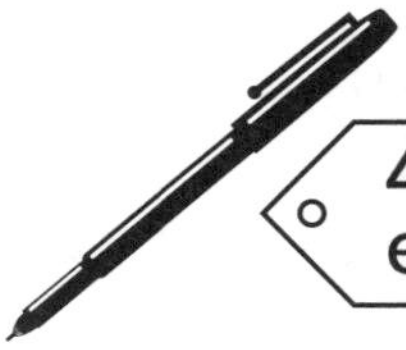   48p each 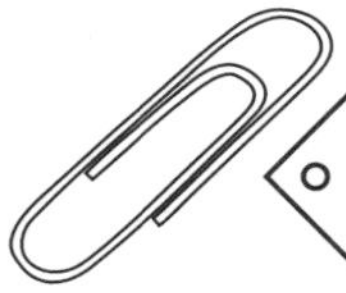   32p each

Lexi has £2 to spend.

She wants to buy a ruler, 2 pens and a giant paperclip.

Does she have enough money? Explain your answer.

4 Work out the total cost of buying a carrot and an onion.

The total cost of buying a carrot and onion is ☐ p.

---

5 A toy train and football cost £18 in total.

A toy train and 2 footballs cost £25 in total.

What is the cost of a football?

The football costs £ ☐ .

CHALLENGE

Reflect

Which problem did you find the most challenging?
How did you find a solution?

Problem solving – money

1 An ice-lolly costs 84p.

Andy buys 5 ice-lollies.

He pays with a £5 note.

How much change does Andy get?

Andy gets £ ☐ change.

2 Max buys 8 bars of chocolate.

He pays with a £10 note.

Max receives £3·52 change.

a) Explain how you know a bar of chocolate costs less than £1.

_____

_____

b) How much does one bar of chocolate cost?

A bar of chocolate costs £ ☐ .

Remember, you need to change the amount into pence first.

3 Is it cheaper to pay for 6 throws for £1·20 or 6 throws at 25p per throw?

6 throws for £1·20 or 25 pence a throw.

It is cheaper to _____

because _____

_____ .

4 Sofia can travel to work using two taxi companies.

POWER CABS
£3 first km and then
40p for each km after

AI CARS
70p for each km
travelled

Sofia wants to travel 9 km to work.

Which taxi company is the least expensive for Sofia's journey?

Show your working.

The least expensive taxi company for Sofia is _____ .

5

£2·$\boxed{}$ + £$\boxed{}$·75 = £8·42

Work out the missing numbers.

---

6 Amelia wants to buy 5 buns.

Buy 4, get 5th bun free.

CHALLENGE

Amelia says it is cheaper to buy the bag of buns because each bun costs 50p.

60p each

£2·50

Is Amelia correct?_____

Reflect

A single bread roll costs 55p.
It is cheaper to buy a pack of 4 bread rolls than to buy 4 single rolls.
How much would you charge for the 4 pack of rolls? Explain why.

→ Textbook 4C p76

End of unit check

My journal

Ebo wants to add £1·34 and 72p.

Lexi says, 'You cannot add these amounts as they are different units.'

Mo says, 'Lexi is right and we do not know how to add decimals yet.'

Explain to Ebo how he could add these amounts.

_____

_____

_____

_____

_____

_____

_____

Keywords:

pounds, pence, convert, add

Power check

How do you feel about your work in this unit?

Power puzzle

1 A kettle costs twice as much as a toaster.

The toaster and kettle cost £72 in total.

How much does each item cost?

A toaster costs £ ⬚.

A kettle costs £ ⬚.

£72

2 A laptop costs 5 times as much as a radio.

The laptop is £340 more than the radio.

How much does the radio cost?

The radio costs £ ⬚.

3 A pair of speakers costs three times as much as a pair of headphones.

A camera costs £36 more than the pair of speakers.

The total cost of the three items is £155.

How much does each item cost?

Can you put all the objects in order, starting with the least expensive?

A pair of speakers costs £ ⬚.

A pair of headphones costs £ ⬚.

A camera costs £ ⬚.

→ **Textbook 4C p80**

Units of time

1 A space shuttle is counting down to take off.

These timers show the time left in different ways.

Complete each bar model to work out the missing time.

a)

I minute 45 seconds

I minute	45 seconds
☐ seconds	☐ seconds

☐ seconds + ☐ seconds = ☐ seconds

b) 3 HOURS 12 MINUTES

_____ MINUTES

3 hours 12 minutes

I hour	I hour	I hour	12 mins

☐ × ☐ minutes = ☐ minutes

☐ minutes + 12 minutes = ☐ minutes

c)

___ MINUTES ___ SECONDS

157 SECONDS

60 seconds
I minute

157 seconds

☐ minutes ☐ seconds

2 Show how you can use 6 times-table facts to help convert times.

1 × 6 = ☐   1 × 60 = ☐   1 hour = ☐ minutes

2 × 6 = ☐   2 × 60 = ☐   ☐ hours = ☐ minutes

3 × 6 = ☐   3 × 60 = ☐   ☐ hours = ☐ minutes

4 × 6 = ☐   4 × 60 = ☐   ☐ hours = ☐ minutes

10 × 6 = ☐   10 × 60 = ☐   ☐ hours = ☐ minutes

3 Use subtraction to find the length of each film in hours and minutes.

Film	Length (minutes)
Lift Off!	135
Escape from Saturn	95
Star Voyager	145

The first film has been done for you.

a) Lift Off!

```
      135 minutes
  −    60 minutes  (1 hour)
  ─────────────────
  =    75 minutes
  −    60 minutes  (1 hour)
  ─────────────────
  =    15 minutes

= 2 hours and
  15 minutes
```

b) Escape from Saturn

c) Star Voyager

4 The winner of the London Marathon finished in 2 hours and 5 minutes.

Ella's dad completed the race in 4 hours and 15 minutes.

How many minutes after the winner did Ella's dad finish the race?

Ella's dad finished the marathon ☐ minutes after the winner.

5 Tom's kitchen tap drips once every second.

CHALLENGE

He puts a bowl underneath it to catch the water.

How many drops will be in the bowl after 1 hour?

Show your working.

Reflect

Explain how to work out the number of hours and minutes in 152 minutes.

Units of time ②

1 Complete the bar models to convert the units of time.

a)

21 days		
☐ days	☐ days	☐ days

$21 \div$ ☐ days $=$ ☐ weeks

The orange juice should be used within ☐ weeks.

b)

3 weeks and 5 days

☐ week	☐ week	☐ week	☐ days
☐ days	☐ days	☐ days	☐ days

$3 \times$ ☐ days $+$ ☐ days $=$ ☐ days

The parcel should be delivered in ☐ days.

c)

36 months

☐ years

Suitable for children over 36 months.

The toy is suitable for children over ☐ years old.

2 Draw lines to match the lengths of time.

4 years   about 30 weeks

12 weeks   730 days

2 years   48 days

6 weeks 6 days   48 months

7 months   84 days

3

How many weeks are there in 53 days?

There are 7 days in a week. 53 × 7 equals 371 weeks.

Lee

Explain the mistake that Lee has made. _____

_____

_____

4 Complete the calculations.

a) 5 weeks + 13 days = 6 weeks ☐ days

b) 38 months − 2 years = ☐ months

5 Complete the sentences. To find the number of ...

months in a number of years, _____ by ☐ .

years in a number of months, _____ by ☐ .

days in a number of weeks, _____ by ☐ .

weeks in a number of days, _____ by ☐ .

6 How old are you in years, weeks and days?

CHALLENGE

☐ years, ☐ weeks and ☐ days.

How many days old are you?

I am ☐ days old.

Reflect

A baby is 20 months old. How long ago (in years and months) was it born?

I can find the answer by _____

_____

_____ .

→ Textbook 4C p88

Converting times

 Draw these digital times on the analogue clocks.

a) 1:31 am   **b)** 2:42 pm   **c)** 3:53 pm   **d)** 4:04 am

   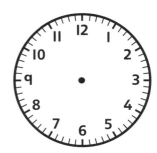

2

The digital time is 11:12.

Emma

The digital time is 11:58.

Max

What is the correct digital time?_____

What mistake has Emma made?

_____

_____

What mistake has Max made?

_____

_____

3 Here are some extracts from a spy's diary. Convert each time into analogue and digital.

a) Catch the plane at twelve minutes past 2 in the morning.

[:] _____

b) Meet Agent X at quarter to 1 in the afternoon.

[:] _____

c) Crack the code by seventeen minutes past 6 in the evening.

[:] _____

4 Kate says, 'It is quarter to 10. My digital clock time has a 9 digit in it. My analogue clock shows the minute hand pointing to the number 9, but they both represent different things!'

Explain what Kate means.

In the digital time, the 9 represents _____

_____ .

In the analogue time, the minute hand pointing to the 9 represents

_____

_____ .

5 It is the afternoon. A digital time contains a 3, a 6 and a 5.

What are four possible times it could be?

Convert each time into an analogue time.

CHALLENGE

Reflect

Explain how to convert an analogue 12-hour time into a digital time.

To convert from analogue into digital, I would _____

_____

_____ .

Converting times ❷

1 What would each time look like on an analogue and 24-hour digital clock?

a) 1:05 am

b) seven o'clock in the evening

c) 11:41 pm

d) 8:28 am

e) two minutes past midnight

 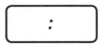

2 Convert these 24-hour digital times into analogue times.

a) 00:00

b) 13:42

c) 20:16

d) 09:51

3 These 24-hour times have all been written incorrectly.

Write each time correctly. Explain the mistakes.

a) 3:42 [:]

_____

_____

b) 15:42 pm [:]

_____

_____

4 Max is going shopping. His watch shows 24-hour times.

His mum says, 'It is now 2:17 pm. I will meet you outside the sports shop in an hour and a half.'

What time will Max's watch show when he has to meet his mum?

Max's watch will show [:].

5 Write down ten 24-hour times where the four digits add up to 8 each time.

Convert your times into 12-hour times.

For example, 05:21 → 5:21 am

CHALLENGE

	24-hour time	12-hour time
1		
2		
3		
4		
5		

	24-hour time	12-hour time
6		
7		
8		
q		
10		

Reflect

Explain how to change between 12-hour and 24-hour clock times.

- _____
- _____
- _____
- _____

→ Textbook 4C p96

Problem solving – units of time

 Two teams of explorers raced each other to be the first to climb to the top of a mountain.

They completed four different stages until they reached the top.

This is a record of their climbs.

Team	Stage 1	Stage 2	Stage 3	Stage 4
Team A	1 week 2 days	2 weeks	1 week 4 days	2 weeks 1 day
Team B	10 days	13 days	11 days	17 days

a) Who completed Stage 1 first?

Team _____ was the first to complete Stage 1. It took ☐ days.

b) How long did it take Team B to complete Stages 1 and 2 altogether?

It took ☐ weeks and ☐ days altogether for Team B to complete Stages 1 and 2.

c) Which team reached the summit first? By how many days?

Show your working.

Team _____ reached the summit ☐ days before Team _____ .

2 The table shows some athletics world records. Convert the times into a different unit of measurement.

Event	World record	Convert to			
Men's 800 m	100 seconds	☐ minutes		☐ seconds	
Women's 1,500 m	230 seconds	☐ minutes		☐ seconds	
Men's 3,000 m	440 seconds	☐ minutes		☐ seconds	
Women's 20 km walk	75 minutes	☐ hours		☐ minutes	
Men's 50 km walk	212 minutes	☐ hours		☐ minutes	

Use this space to show your working.

3 The classroom clock is analogue. Zac's digital watch shows 24-hour times.

It is twenty to 3 in the afternoon. What do the clock and the watch look like?

71

4 Here is information about the ages of four babies.

Abdul	Ben	Cerys	Dan
24 months	1 year 10 months	3 months older than Ben	4 months younger than Cerys

Write the babies' names in order from youngest to oldest.

---

5 A bus takes 95 minutes to travel from the bus station to the retail park. It arrives at the retail park at 14:02. What time did it leave the bus station?

CHALLENGE

The bus left the bus station at ☐ : ☐ .

Reflect

Write how you would convert 108 months into years. Explain it to a partner.

→ Textbook 4C p100

End of unit check

My journal

How long have you been alive? Is this more, equal to or less than 100 months?

Use this space to show your working.

I know I have been alive more / the same as / less than 100 months

because _____

_____

_____

Keywords:

convert, months, years, units

Power check

How do you feel about your work in this unit?

Power puzzle

Inside this grid there is one time that does not have an equal pair.

Which one is it?

Try colouring each pair in a different colour to help you spot the odd time out.

If you are working with a partner, take it in turns to colour a pair until you are left with the odd one out.

06:56	3 hours 46 minutes	60 months	(clock showing 11:00)	8 weeks 4 days
01:02	226 minutes	5 years	17:56	4 years 11 months
(clock showing 1:10)	60 days	6:56 am	59 months	13:10

Try making your own puzzle for a partner to solve. Remember that each time must be part of a pair – apart from one!

Charts and tables ❶

1 Kieron and Amy collect 'Ninja Man' collecting cards.

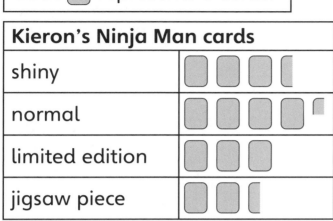

Each ▢ represents 8 cards.

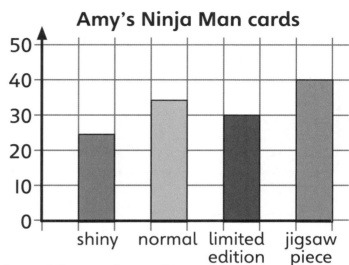

Amy's Ninja Man cards

a) How many jigsaw piece cards does Kieron have?

Each ▢ represents ☐ . Each ▍ represents ☐ .

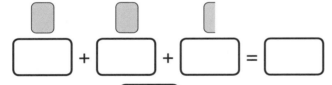

☐ + ☐ + ☐ = ☐

Kieron has ☐ jigsaw piece cards.

b) How many normal cards does Kieron have?

Each ▍ represents ☐ .

Kieron has ☐ normal cards.

c) How many shiny cards does Amy have?

Amy has ☐ shiny cards.

2 Complete these sentences.

Number of books read during Year 4

	Otis	Evie	Gracie
non-fiction	7	10	8
fiction	22	20	23
poetry	3	5	6
Total:	32	35	37

Evie read ☐ fiction books.

Gracie read ☐ non-fiction books.

Otis read ☐ poetry books.

Gracie read ☐ books in total.

3 Use the information in the table to create a pictogram for the number of non-fiction books read.

Number of non-fiction books read

Each ■ represents 2 books.

	Number of books read
Otis	
Evie	
Gracie	

4 Complete the missing information.

Number of pages read in one term

Milo	☐
Otis	4,500
Grace	☐
Finlay	2,250

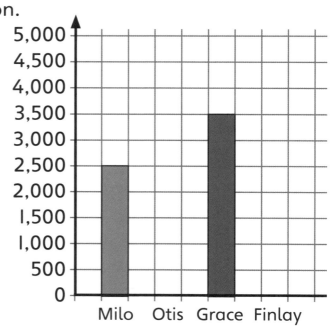

5 Complete the pictogram and bar chart.

CHALLENGE

Number of class points earnt last term:

	Year 3	Year 4	Year 5	Year 6
Earth	275	225	300	200
Air	350	400	225	375
Fire	325	375	300	350
Water	450	450	300	350

Number of class points per team in Year 4

Each ● represents ▢ points.

	Items
Earth	
Air	
Fire	
Water	●●●● ◖

Total number of class points earnt last term

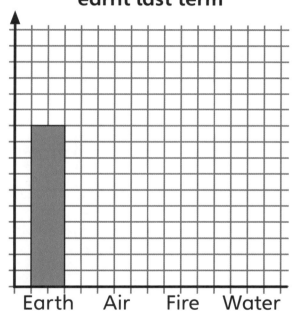

Earth   Air   Fire   Water

Reflect

Which is the best way to display data? Discuss with a partner and write your answers.

→ Textbook 4C p108

Charts and tables ❷

1

Each ◠ represents 6 marbles.

Number of marbles won in December	
Tom	◠ ◠
Alice	◠ ◠ ◠ ◡
Otis	◠ ◠ ◡
Gracie	◠ ◡

Number of marbles won in May

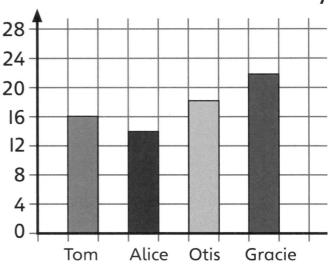

a) How many marbles did Alice win in December and May altogether?

⬚ + ⬚ = ⬚

Alice won ⬚ marbles in December and May.

b) How many more marbles did Otis win in May compared to Alice?

Otis won ⬚ marbles in May.

Alice won ⬚ marbles in May.

⬚ – ⬚ = ⬚

Otis won ⬚ more marbles in May than Alice.

c) How many marbles did the children win in May altogether?

The children won ⬚ marbles in May.

2 This table shows the number of visitors to the History Museum and the Science Museum over three days.

Complete the table.

Number of visitors

	History Museum	Science Museum	Total
Saturday	625		1,425
Sunday	745	725	
Monday		390	780

3 Tom and Sarah are playing video games. Use the information below to complete the table, then complete a bar chart showing the scores for Sarah.

Sarah scored 450 more on Vault Explorer than Tom.

Tom scored 250 more on Climbing Road than he did on Space Raiders.

Number of points earned

	Space Raiders	Vault Explorer	Climbing Road
Sarah	700		850
Tom	550	200	

Number of points scored by Sarah

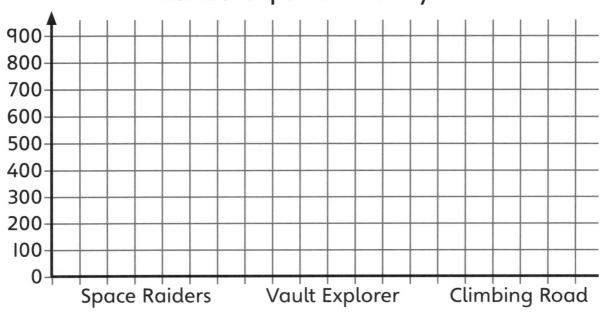

4 The bar chart shows the number of children who have a packed lunch and a hot lunch each day.

Each child has to have a packed lunch or a hot lunch.

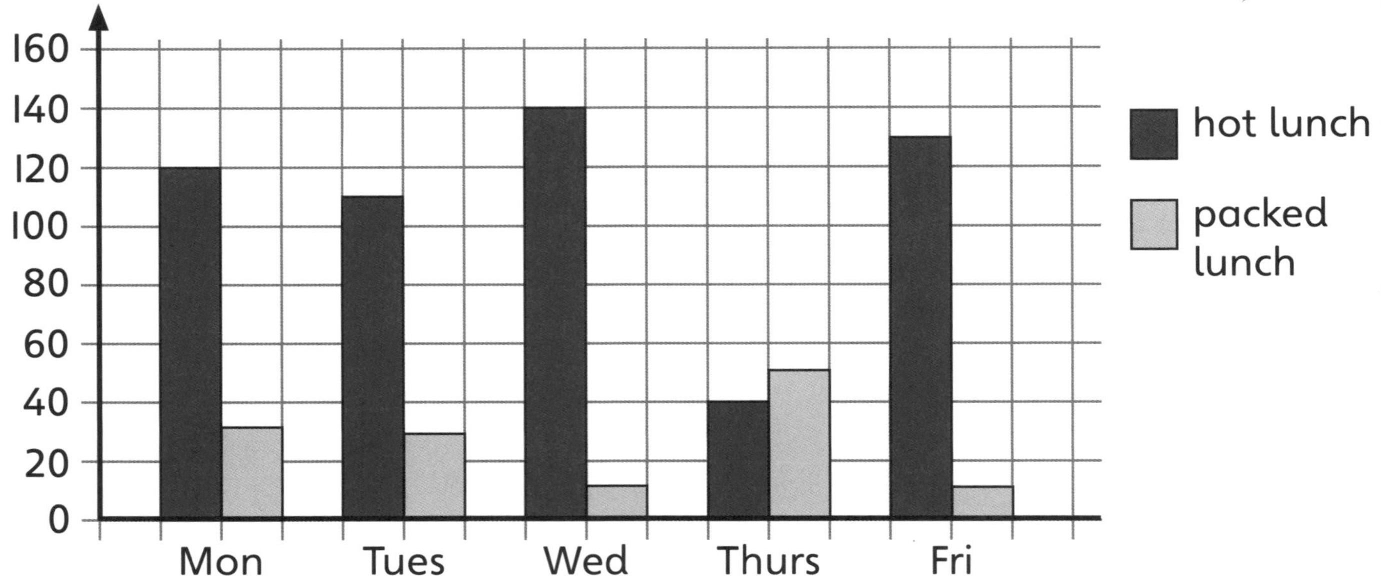

CHALLENGE

■ hot lunch

□ packed lunch

a) There are 160 children in the school.

How many children were off school on Friday? ☐

b) Which day was there the greatest difference between the number of children who had a hot lunch and those that had a packed lunch? _____ What was the difference? ☐

Reflect

What types of graph do you know? Which do you prefer? Why?

- _____
- _____
- _____

Line graphs ❶

❶

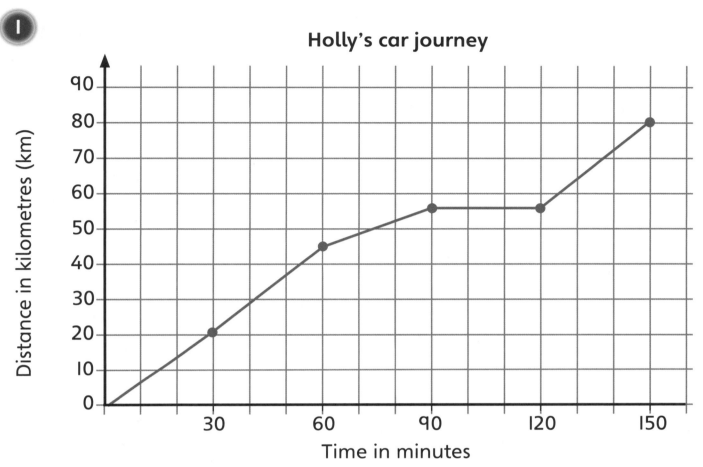

Holly's car journey

a) How many kilometres has Holly travelled after 30 minutes?

Holly has travelled ⬚ kilometres after 30 minutes.

b) How many kilometres has she travelled after 90 minutes?

Holly has travelled ⬚ kilometres after 90 minutes.

c) How long did it take Holly to travel 45 kilometres?

It took Holly ⬚ minutes to travel 45 kilometres.

d) The total length of the journey was 80 kilometres.

It took Holly ⬚ minutes to complete the journey.

2

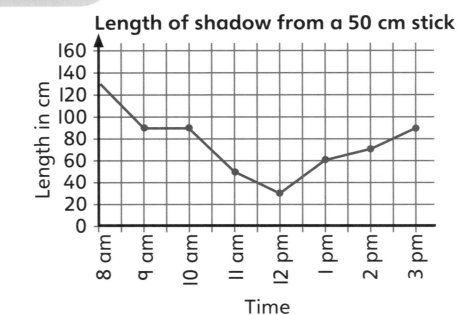

Length of shadow from a 50 cm stick

a) What was the length of the shadow at 8:30 am?

The shadow was ☐ cm at 8:30 am.

b) When was the shadow 30 cm?

The shadow was 30 cm at _____ .

3 Complete the sentences.

The shadow was the longest at _____ . It was ☐ cm long.

The shadow was the shortest at _____ . It was ☐ cm long.

The shadow was the same length at both _____ and _____ .

4 Would a line graph be a good way to present this data? Explain your answer.

_____

_____

_____

_____

People's favourite colour

blue	12
yellow	10
green	16
red	8

5

Distance travelled during a car journey

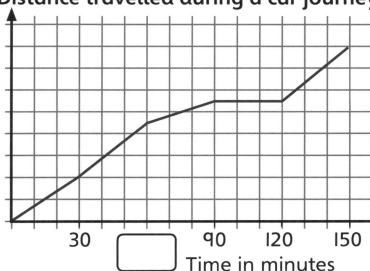

Distance in miles

30   90   120   150

Time in minutes

Car journey

Time	30 minutes		90 minutes	120 minutes	150 minutes
Distance		45 miles			

a) Complete the table and the axes on the line graph.

b) When was the car stuck in a traffic jam? Explain your answer.

_____

_____

Reflect

When would you use a line graph instead of a bar chart?

_____

_____

_____

Line graphs ❷

1 An open container was put out in the rain.

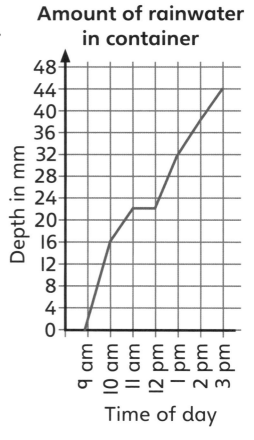

Amount of rainwater in container

a) How much more water was in the container at 11 am than at 10 am?

There was ⬚ mm more water in the container at 11 am.

b) Complete the sentence.

It took ⬚ hours for the water level to increase from 22 mm to 32 mm.

Explain why it took this long.

_____

_____

How do you know?

_____

_____

2 **a)** How many steps did Evie take during the day?

Evie took [   ] steps during the day.

b) How many steps did Evie take between 12 pm and 3 pm?

c) How long did Evie take to go from 500 to 1,500 steps?

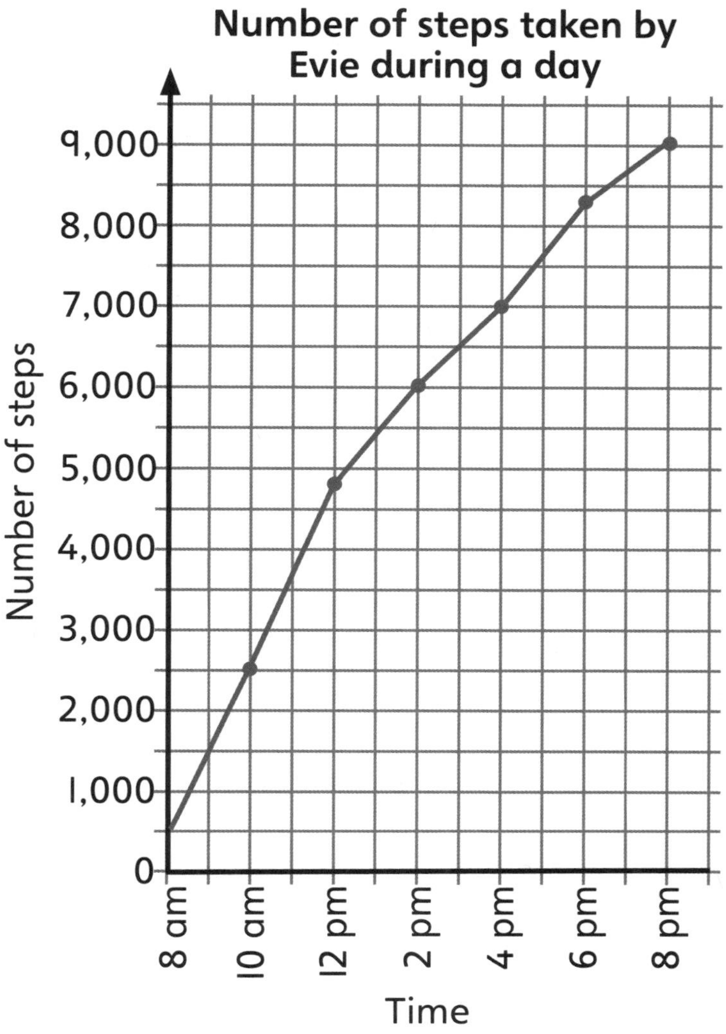

Number of steps taken by Evie during a day

3 Max hits a golf ball.

The graph shows the height of the ball off the ground at different times.

What is the greatest height the ball reaches?

_____

_____

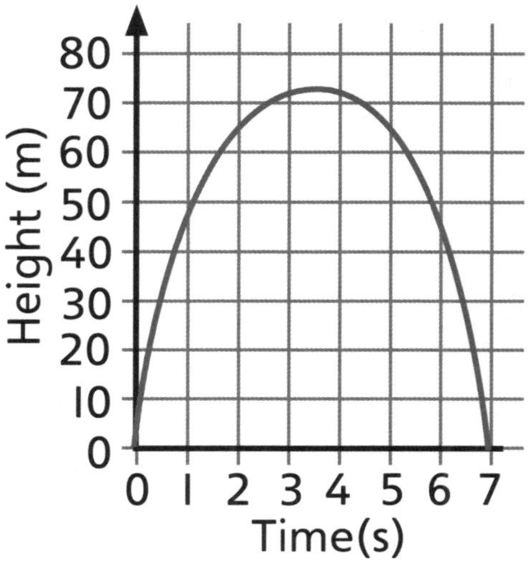

How do you know?

_____

_____

4 Write five statements about the graph.
Use the words below to help you.

CHALLENGE

warmest, coldest, difference, same,
different, more than, less than

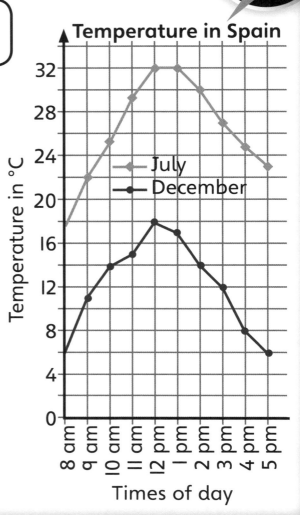

Temperature in Spain

_____

_____

_____

_____

_____

_____

_____

_____

_____

Reflect

Write some reflections on this lesson.

- One important thing I am going to remember when looking at
- line graph data is
-
- _____ .

Problem solving – graphs

1 **a)** How many more steps did Lily and Maisie take compared to Tom and Kieron?

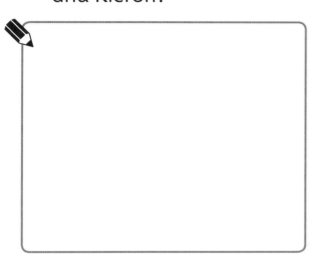

Number of steps taken on one day

Tom   Lily   Maisie   Kieron

Lily and Maisie took ⬚ more steps than Tom and Kieron.

b) Gracie walked 1,500 more steps than Maisie. How many steps did Gracie walk?

Gracie walked ⬚ steps.

2

Temperatures in June

	Highest temperature	Lowest temperature
London	23 °C	12 °C
Cardiff	19 °C	12 °C
Belfast	30 °C	15 °C
Edinburgh	28 °C	12 °C

a) What is the difference between the highest and lowest temperature in Cardiff? ⬚ °C

b) Which city's highest temperature is double its lowest temperature? _____

c) Which city has the largest difference between its highest and lowest temperature? _____

87

3 Otis went on a sponsored walk.
He took two breaks.

Distance walked

a) Write 'first' or 'last' to make this sentence correct.

Otis walked furthest in the

_____ 2 hours of his walk.

b) Explain your answer.

_____

_____

_____

_____

_____

_____

c) Otis raised £6 per kilometre that he walked.

How much money did Otis raise in total for charity between 12 pm and 3 pm?

Otis rasied £ [   ] for charity between 12 pm and 3 pm.

4 Estimate the difference between the population of Glastonbury and Overton.

CHALLENGE

Each ⬤ represents 2,000 people.

Population of different towns in the UK	
Windermere	⬤⬤◗
Twyford	⬤⬤⬤◖
Glastonbury	⬤⬤⬤⬤◢
Battle	⬤⬤⬤

Population

| | Overton | Spixworth | Meophan | Cranleigh |

Reflect

Look at the pictogram and bar chart in question 4.

Write two questions for a partner to answer based on these graphs.

→ Textbook 4C p124

End of unit check

My journal

This line graph shows the price of Tom's toy car that he is selling in an auction.

Write three bits of information you can tell from the line graph. Use some of the words below to help you.

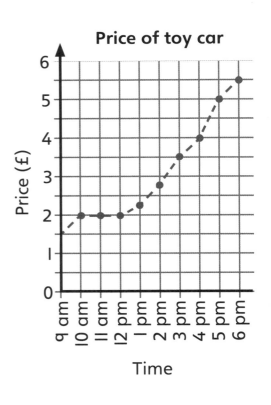

Price of toy car

> **Keywords:**
>
> more than, altogether, total, less than, compared to

_____

_____

_____

_____

_____

_____

_____

Power check

How do you feel about your work in this unit?

Power puzzle

1 Evie measured her height and the height of three other people in her class. She created bar charts of the data.

Use the bar charts and the clues below to help you complete the missing information.

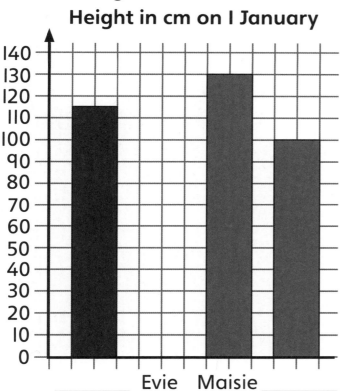

Height in cm on 1 January

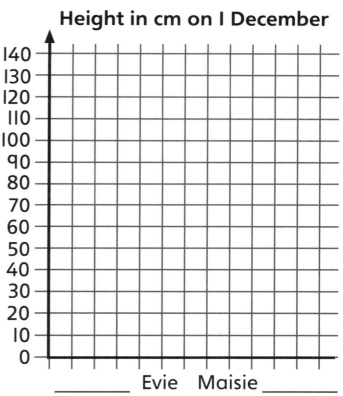

Height in cm on 1 December

Maisie was 130 cm tall in January and grew 5 cm between January and December.

In December, Maisie was the same height as Evie.

Raj was 15 cm shorter than the next shortest child in January.

Evie grew 15 cm between January and December.

Finlay was 15 cm shorter than Maisie in January, but only 10 cm shorter than Maisie in December.

Raj was 10 cm shorter than Finlay in December.

91

Measure your height and the height of three other people in your class. Draw a pictogram and bar chart to represent the heights.

Identifying angles

1 **a)** Tick the acute angles.

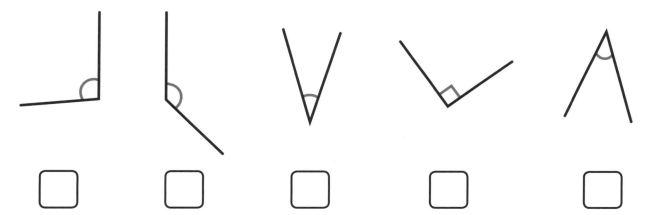

b) Tick the right angles.

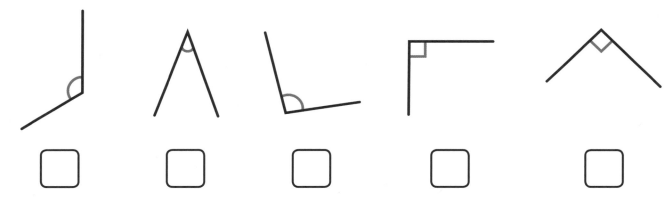

c) Tick the obtuse angles.

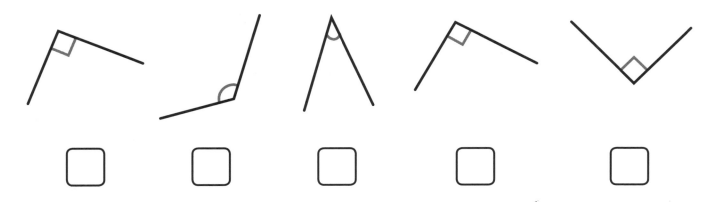

2 Draw a right angle, an acute angle and an obtuse angle.

3 Circle the shape which is in the wrong place.

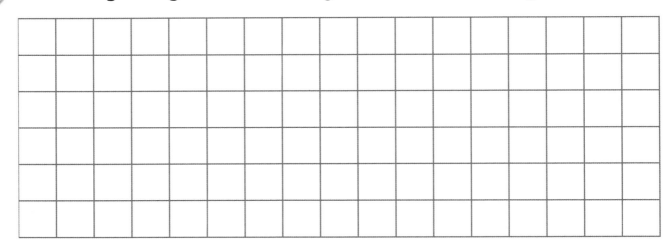

	Shapes with an acute angle	Shapes without an acute angle
Shapes with an obtuse angle	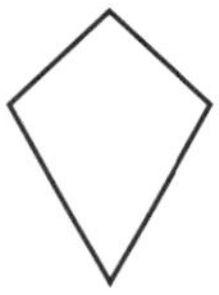 ◇	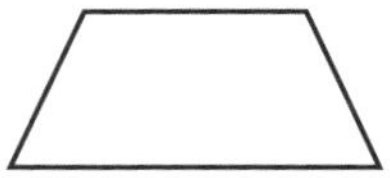 ⬡
Shapes without an obtuse angle	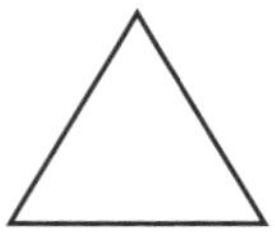 △	▢

4 Which vertices of the kite will fit into this right angle and why?

_____

_____

_____

_____

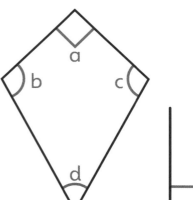

5 Philippa is standing in the middle of the field. What object could she be facing if she turns an acute angle in either direction?

_____

Reflect

Write definitions of an acute, an obtuse and a right angle.

An acute angle _____

_____ .

An obtuse angle _____

_____ .

A right angle _____

_____ .

→ **Textbook 4C p132**

Comparing and ordering angles

1 **a)** Compare and order these angles from largest to smallest.

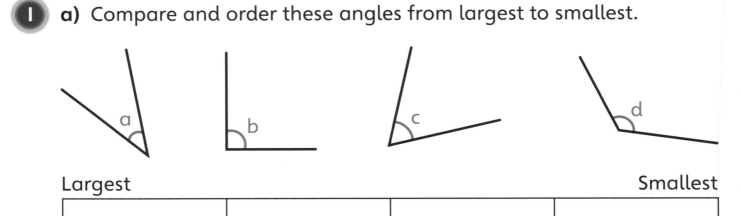

Largest   Smallest

b) Compare and order these angles from smallest to largest.

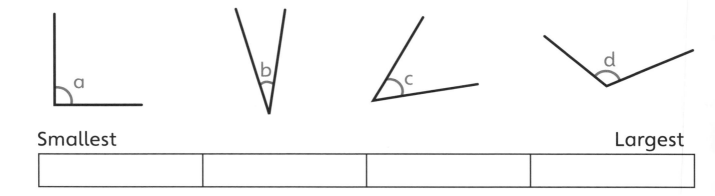

Smallest   Largest

c) Compare and order these angles from largest to smallest.

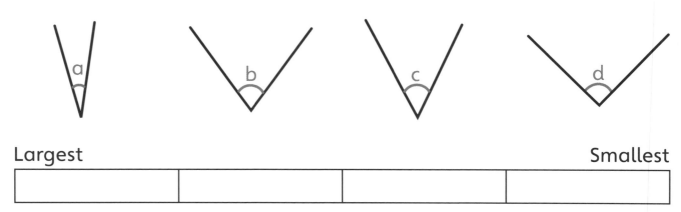

Largest   Smallest

2 **a)** Compare and order these shapes in order of the size of their interior angle. Use a right angle measurer to help.

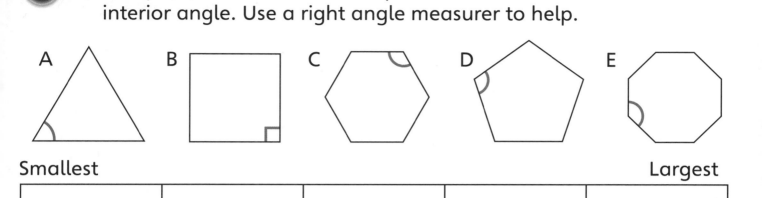

Smallest   Largest

b) Do you notice a pattern between the type of shape and the size of the angles? Explain what you have noticed.

_____

_____

_____

_____

3 Finish drawing these angles so they are in ascending order of size.

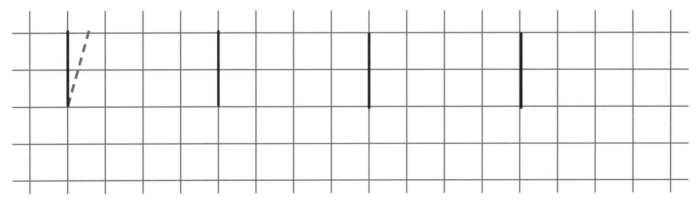

Can you include all three types of angle?

4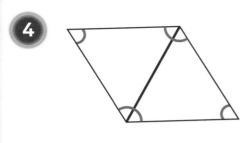

CHALLENGE

Two acute angles can make an obtuse angle.

Is what Mo says always sometimes or never true? Explain and use diagrams to show your ideas.

Reflect

How can you use what you know about right angles to help you identify acute and obtuse angles?

→ **Textbook 4C p136**

Identifying regular and irregular shapes

1 **a)** Circle the regular shapes.

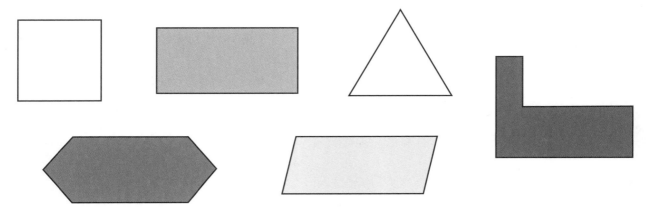

b) Circle the irregular shapes.

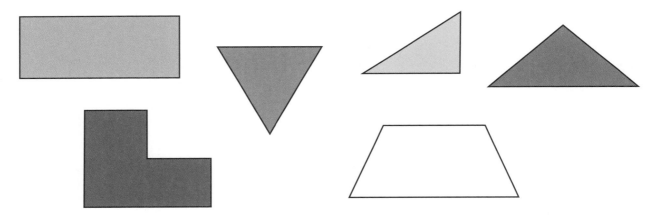

c) Colour the regular shapes blue and the irregular shapes red.

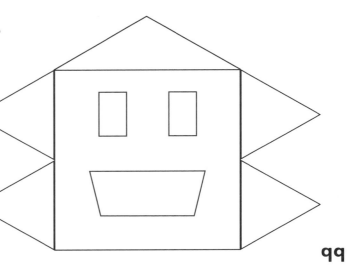

2 Draw two different regular 4-sided shapes.

3 Draw a regular and an irregular 6-sided shape.

4 Reena is describing a picture. Which one is she describing?

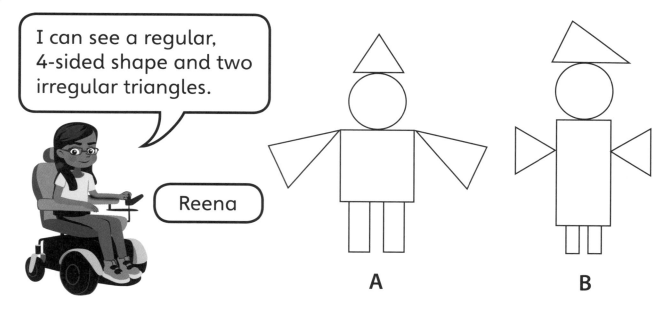

I can see a regular, 4-sided shape and two irregular triangles.

Reena

A

B

Reena is describing picture _____ .

100

5 Which of these shapes can be joined to create a regular hexagon? Circle the shapes that can be used. Draw two different solutions.

CHALLENGE

I think I will need to use some shapes more than once.

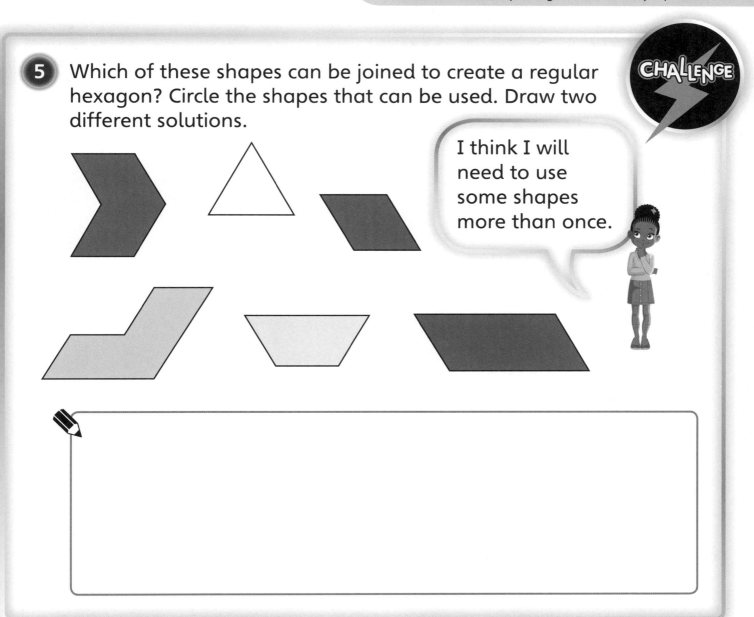

Reflect

Explain how you know whether or not a shape is irregular.

→ Textbook 4C p140

Classifying triangles

1 **a)** Circle all the equilateral triangles.

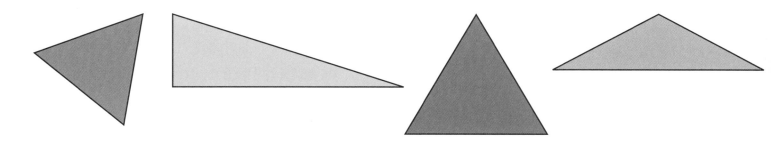

b) Circle all the isosceles triangles.

c) Circle all the scalene triangles.

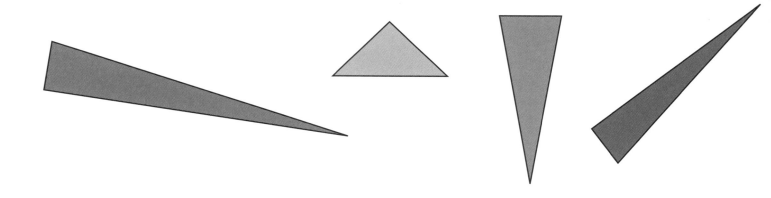

2 Colour this rug using these colours for the different types of triangle.

Equilateral: Red

Isosceles: Yellow

Scalene: Blue

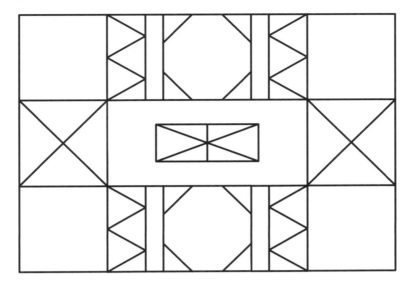

3 Draw two lines on the square to create an isosceles triangle and two right-angled triangles.

4 Sort the triangles below into the correct part of the table.

	2 or 3 equal sides	No equal sides
2 or 3 equal angles		
No equal angles		

I wonder if it is possible to have a triangle in every box.

A 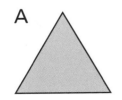 B 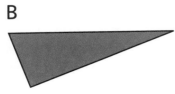 C   D

5 How many isosceles triangles can you find?

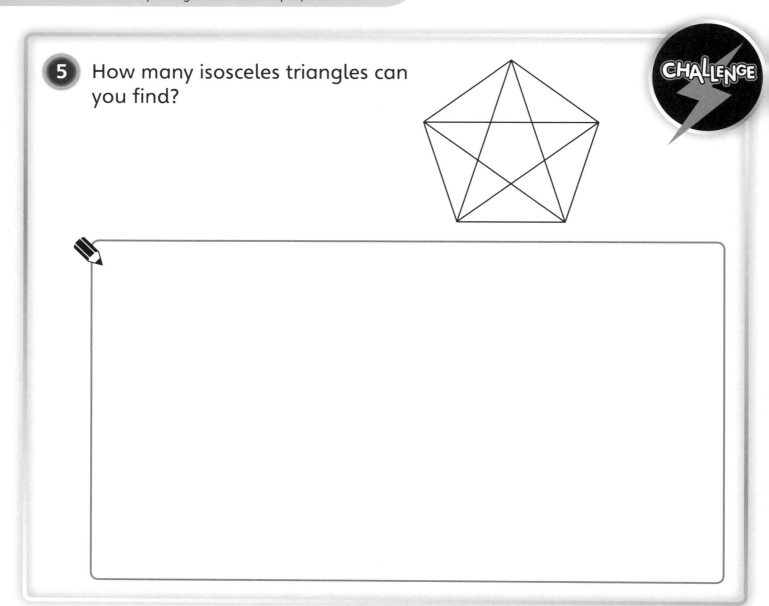

CHALLENGE

Reflect

Explain to your partner how each type of triangle is different to the others.

Classifying and comparing quadrilaterals

1 **a)** Circle all the quadrilaterals.

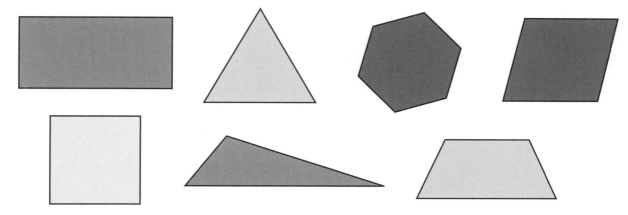

b) Circle all the regular quadrilaterals.

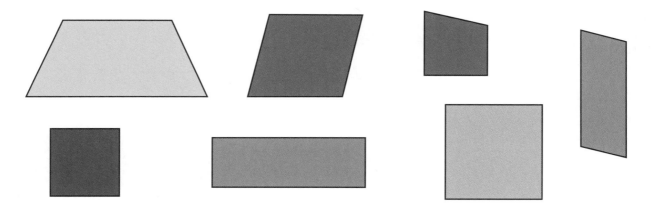

c) Circle all the irregular quadrilaterals.

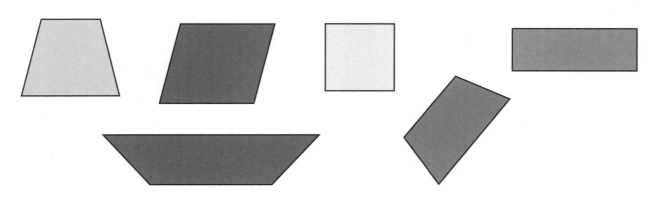

2 Draw two different regular and four different irregular quadrilaterals.

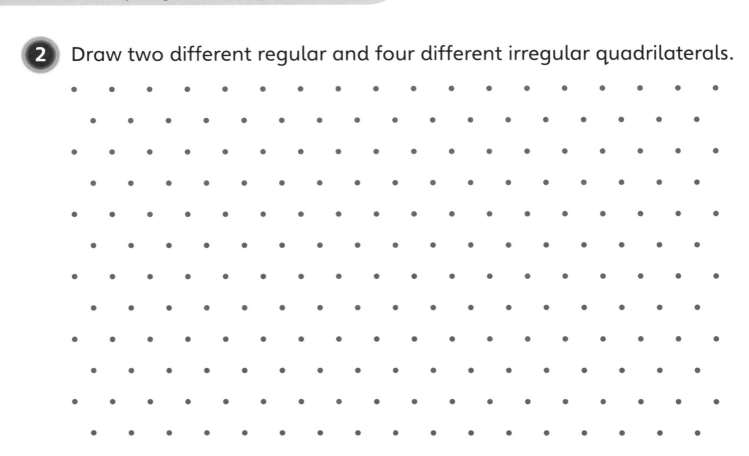

3 Match the names to the shapes.

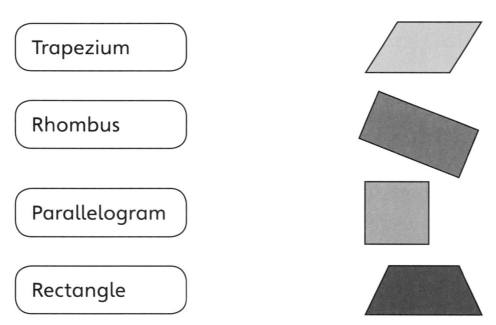

Trapezium

Rhombus

Parallelogram

Rectangle

There is a picture of a square but no label for a square. I wonder what else I can call a square.

4 Draw four different quadrilaterals using the clues below:

- It is irregular.

- It has two acute angles.

- It has two angles greater than a right angle.

- It has two pairs of equal parallel sides.

Reflect

Explain why a square can always be identified as a rhombus but not all rhombuses are squares.

→ Textbook 4C p148

Deducing facts about shapes

1 **a)** Circle the shapes used to make the shape on the left.

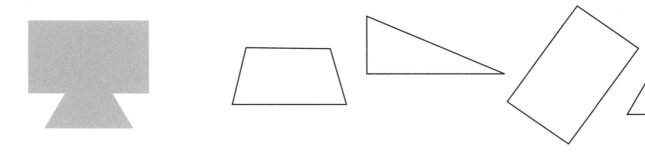

b) Circle the shapes used to make the shape on the left.

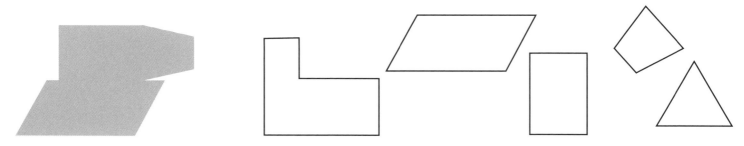

c) Circle the shapes used to make the shape on the left.

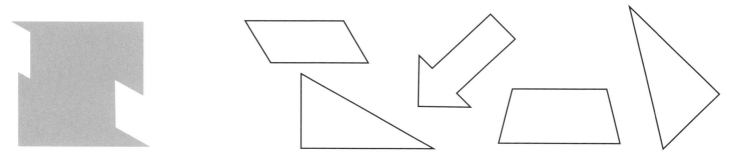

d) Circle the shapes used to make the shape on the left.

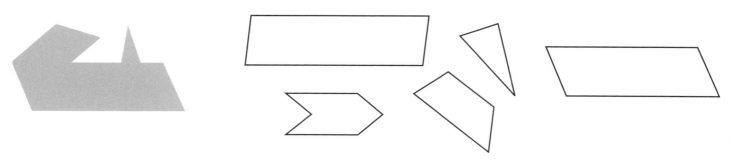

2 What shapes can be made by overlapping two isosceles triangles?

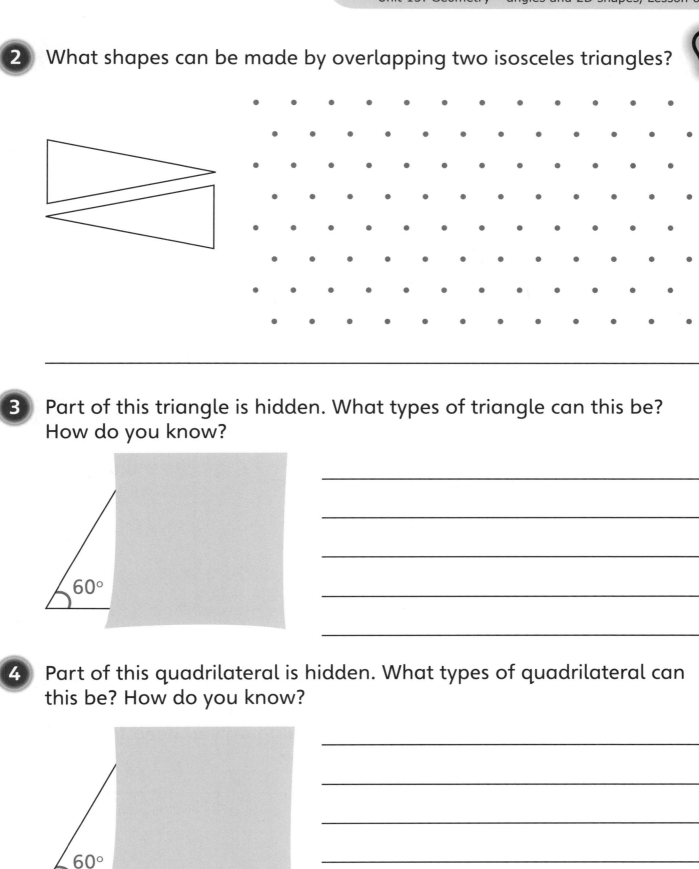

_____

3 Part of this triangle is hidden. What types of triangle can this be? How do you know?

60°

_____

_____

_____

_____

4 Part of this quadrilateral is hidden. What types of quadrilateral can this be? How do you know?

60°

_____

_____

_____

_____

_____

CHALLENGE

5 Complete the headings for the table below.

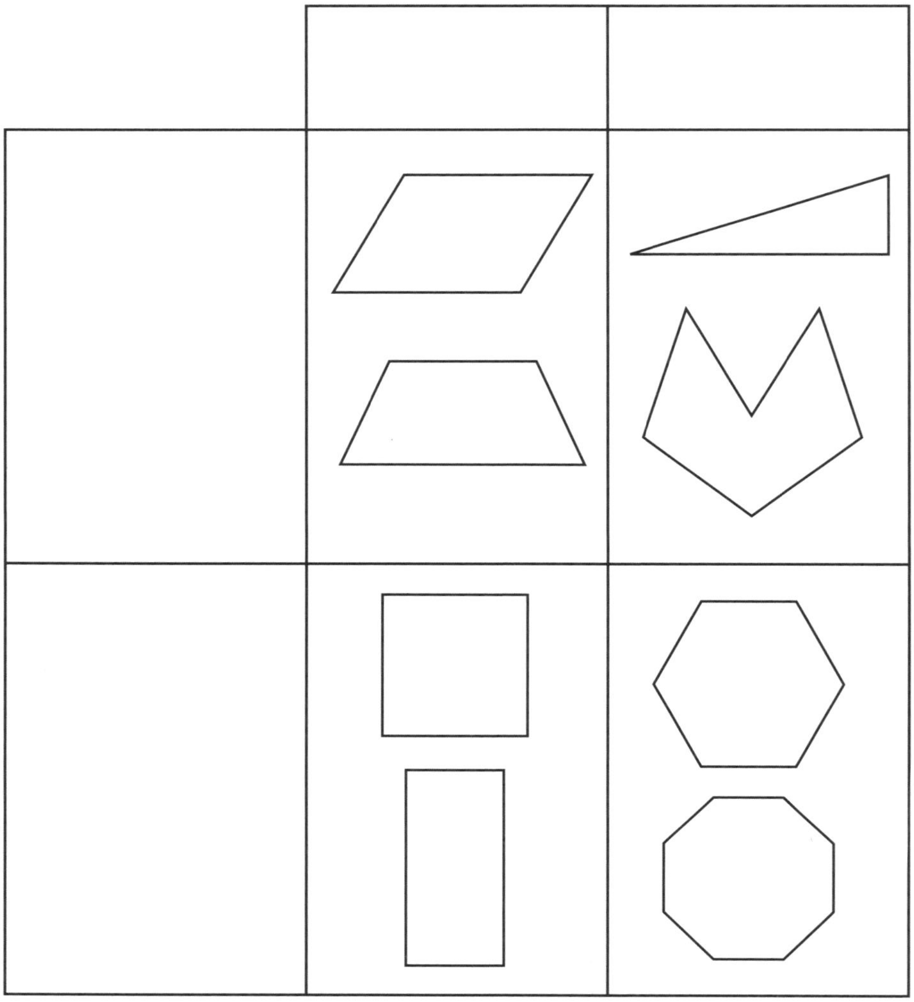

I will think about the facts I know about these shapes and their angles.

Reflect

To know what type of polygon you are looking at, you need to consider …

Lines of symmetry inside a shape

1 Find and draw all the lines of symmetry in these shapes.

a) Isosceles triangle

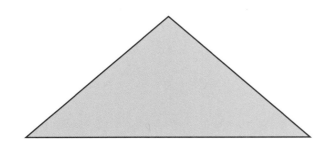

c) Regular octagon

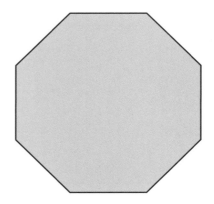

b) Rectangle

d) Irregular octagon

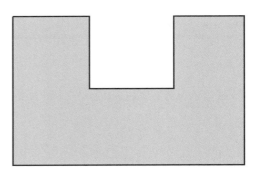

2 Find and draw the lines of symmetry in these flags.

3 Draw the shapes in the table.

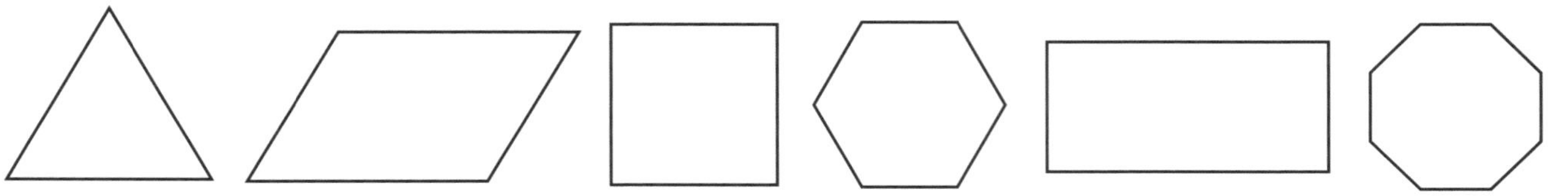

	Regular	**Irregular**
4 or more lines of symmetry		
Fewer than 4 lines of symmetry		

4 Draw an irregular hexagon that has two lines of symmetry.

CHALLENGE

5 Draw three different shapes:

a) One with exactly one line of symmetry.

b) One with exactly two lines of symmetry.

c) One with exactly three lines of symmetry.

Reflect

How many lines of symmetry are there in a circle? Explain your thinking to your partner.

113

→ **Textbook 4C p156**

Lines of symmetry outside a shape

1 Are these sequences of shapes symmetric patterns?

Pattern	Symmetric	Not symmetric
a) ○ □ △ □ ○		
b) □ ⋈ △ ▯		
c) ⋈ ⋈ □ ⋈ ⋈		

I will use a mirror to see if I can find lines of symmetry.

2 Draw the lines of reflective symmetry for this pattern.

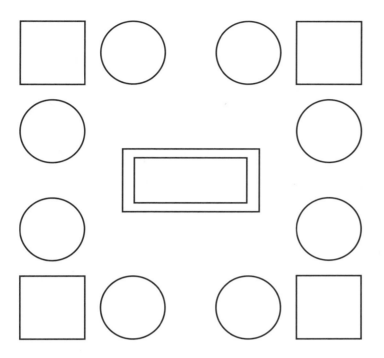

I will look for vertical, horizontal and diagonal lines of symmetry.

3 Draw the lines of symmetry for this pattern.

I think there are lines of symmetry inside and outside of the shapes.

4 Lexi has created a symmetric pattern for her wallpaper. She has made some errors. Find and circle them. Use diagrams to show your ideas.

Reflect

Show two different designs for a symmetric pattern.

Completing a symmetric figure

1 Draw lines to match the start of each pattern with the correct end.

2 Complete these symmetric patterns.

a)

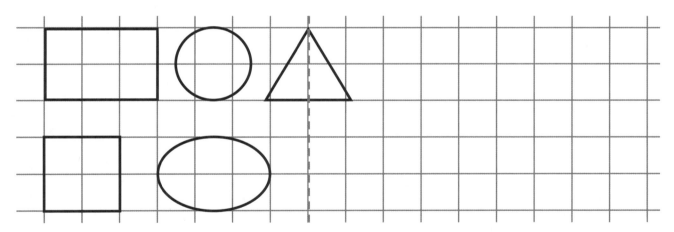

b)

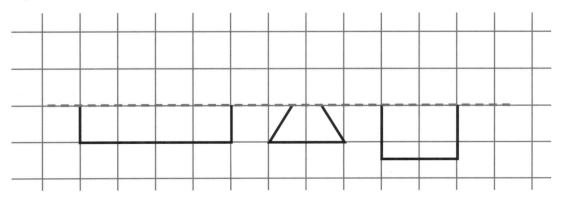

117

3 Complete this symmetric picture.

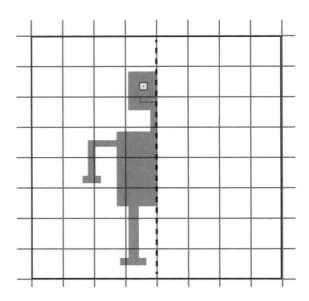

4 Complete this symmetric pattern.

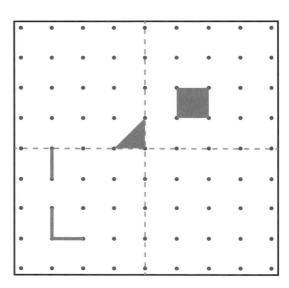

5 Complete this symmetric pattern.

I wonder what the pattern would be like if I added some more shapes.

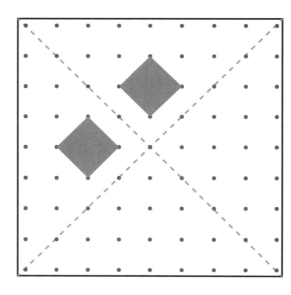

6 Add two more sides to this shape so that it has only one line of symmetry

7 Complete a symmetric pattern.

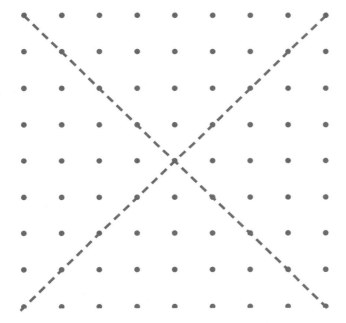

Reflect

Draw a symmetric pattern with two lines of symmetry for your partner to complete.

→ Textbook 4C p164

Completing a symmetric shape

1 Complete the symmetric shapes. Name each shape once you have drawn it.

a)

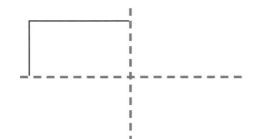

Name of shape: _____

b)

Name of shape: _____

c)

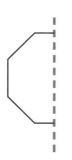

Name of shape: _____

d)

Name of shape: _____

2 What shapes will this symmetric pattern create?

_____

_____

_____

_____

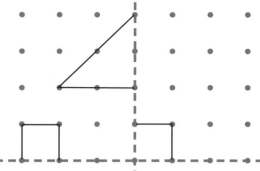

3 Complete the shape.

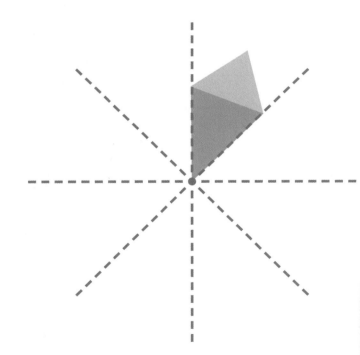

I will have to look closely to make sure I reflect the shapes in all the lines of symmetry.

4 Use these lines of symmetry to create an irregular octagon with at least four obtuse angles.

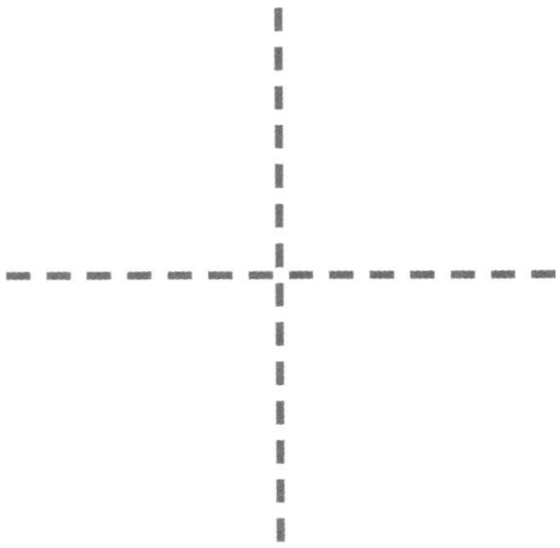

5 You cannot have a shape with exactly two lines of symmetry and an odd number of sides.

CHALLENGE

Alex

Can you disprove Alex's statement? Explain.

_____

_____

_____

_____

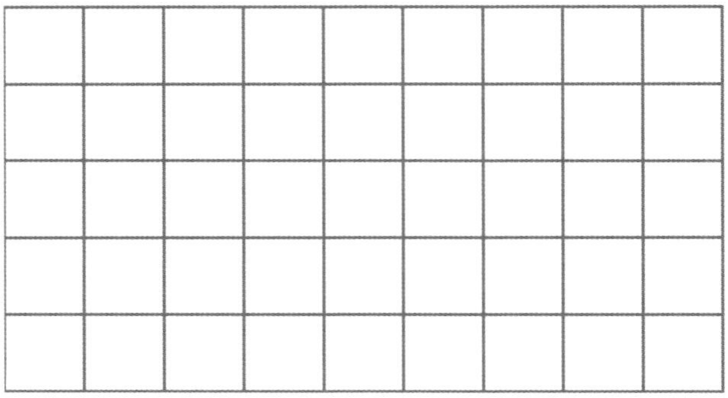

Reflect

When completing a symmetric shape, it is important to …

- _____
- _____
- _____
- _____

→ Textbook 4C p168

End of unit check

My journal

1 Draw **two** straight lines across the hexagon to make two triangles and two quadrilaterals.

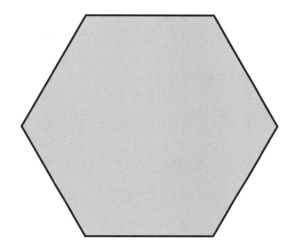

How many solutions can you find?

2 Greg draws a triangle. He says, 'Two of the three angles in my triangle are obtuse.'

Prove why Greg **cannot** be correct.

_____

_____

_____

_____

_____

Power check

How do you feel about your work in this unit?

Power puzzle

Can you fold an A4 piece of paper to make a square?

How about an isosceles triangle or an equilateral triangle?

Show your partner. Can they work out how you did it?

→ Textbook 4C p172

Describing position

1 Use the map to identify places from the information given.

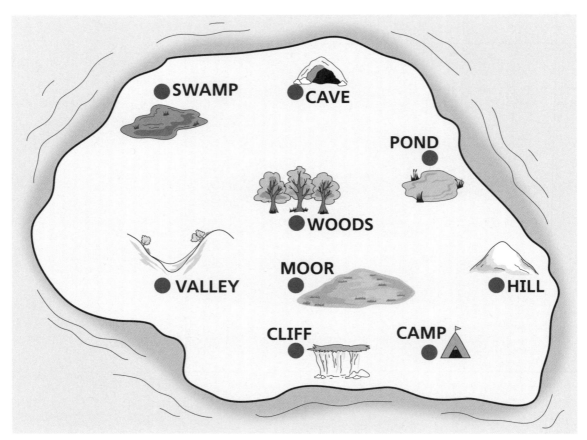

a) This place is next to the moor and close to the camp.

_____

b) This place is in the centre of the map.

_____

c) This place is between the cliff and the cave. It is closer to the cliff than the cave.

_____

d) This is the closest place to the camp.

_____

2 Describe where these places are.

a) The camp _____

_____

b) The cave _____

_____

c) The pond _____

_____

d) The swamp _____

_____

e) The moor _____

_____

f) The cliff _____

_____

3 Imagine drawing a straight line from the cave to the cliff.

Which other places would the line go through?

_____

4

Andy

The woods are exactly half-way between the cave and the moor.

Is Andy correct? Explain your answer.

_____

_____

5 Here is another version of the map.

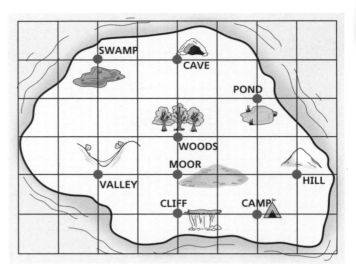

Use this version of the map to describe where some places are. Pass them to a partner to find.

_____

_____

Does this version make it more efficient to say where the places are? Explain your answer.

_____

_____

Reflect

How can maps and grids help you to explain where things are?

_____

_____

_____

_____

Describing position ❷

1 Jamie made a sketch of her garden.

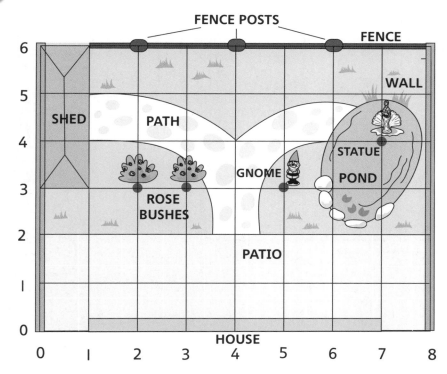

a) What are the coordinates of the statue?

The statue is at ([ ] , [ ]).

b) There is a fence post at (2,6). Where are the other fence posts?

The other fence posts are at ([ ] , [ ]) and ([ ] , [ ]).

c) One of the rose bushes is at (2,3). Where is the other one?

The other rose bush is at ([ ] , [ ]).

2 The coordinates of one corner of the shed are (1,3).

What are the coordinates of the other three corners?

The other corners are at ([ ] , [ ]) , ([ ] , [ ])

and ([ ] , [ ]).

3

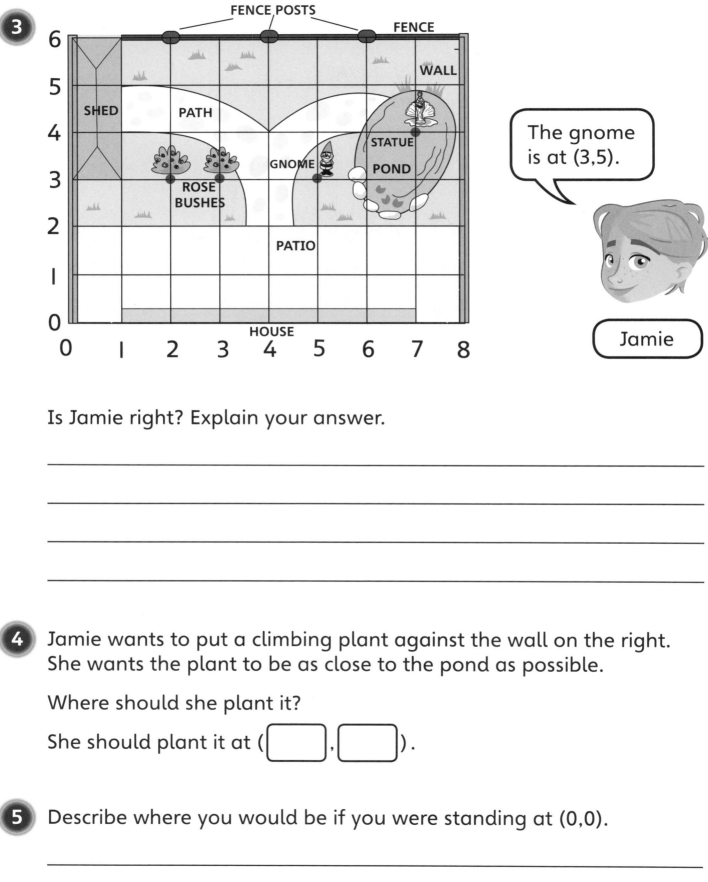

The gnome is at (3,5).

Jamie

Is Jamie right? Explain your answer.

_____

_____

_____

_____

4 Jamie wants to put a climbing plant against the wall on the right. She wants the plant to be as close to the pond as possible.

Where should she plant it?

She should plant it at ([ ] , [ ]).

5 Describe where you would be if you were standing at (0,0).

_____

6 There is a spade in the shed. What could its position be if it is:

a) as far away from the house as possible?   (⬚ , ⬚)

b) as close to the house as possible?   (⬚ , ⬚)

7 Which one of these positions would be a good place to plant a bush? Explain your answer.

CHALLENGE

A (1,4)   B (4,1)   C (4,3)   D (4,5)   E (7,3)

(⬚ , ⬚) because

_____

_____

_____

_____

(2,4) means start at (0,0) and go
2 squares up and then 4 squares right.

Reflect

Do you agree with Ebo? Explain your answer.   Ebo

_____

_____

_____

Drawing on a grid

1 Each of these points is a corner of a different shape.

Here are the coordinates of all of the corners of the shapes. Plot the points, and draw the shapes.

a) (1,2), (2,2), (2,7)

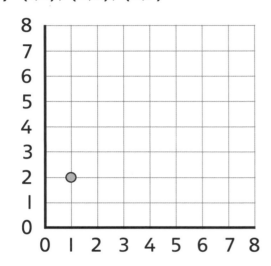

b) (7,1), (7,4), (4,4), (5,1)

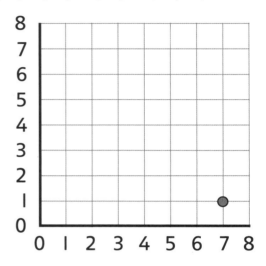

2 Draw these straight-sided shapes on the grid. What shapes are they?

a) Vertices at (1,5), (1,7) and (4,6).

b) Vertices at (1,1), (3,1), (3,4), (2,4) and (1,3).

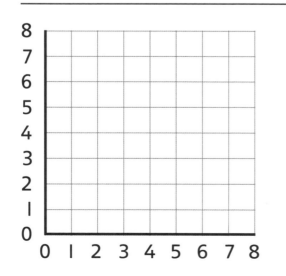

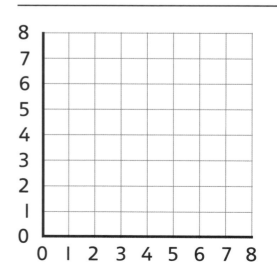

3 Here are the coordinates of some points on two lines.

- Line I: (0,3), (I,3), (2,3), (3,3), (4,3), (5,3), (6,3), (7,3), (8,3)

- Line 2: (5,8), (5,7), (5,6), (5,5), (5,4), (5,3), (5,2), (5,I), (5,0)

a) Can you work out what the lines will look like before you draw them? Write down your prediction.

Line I: _____

_____

Line 2: _____

_____

b) Plot the coordinates and draw the lines.

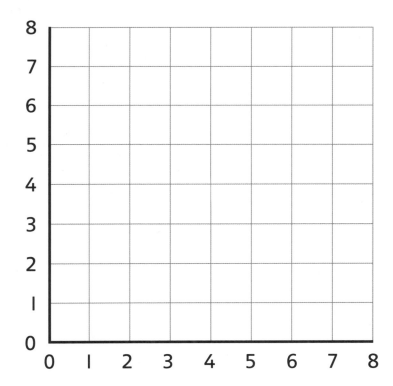

Were your predictions correct?

_____

133

4 **a)** Draw a design for a star shape on this grid.

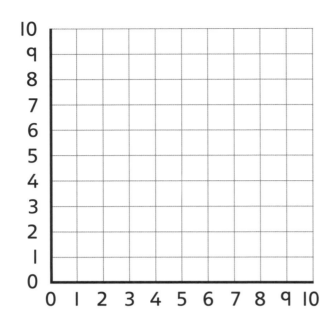

b) Write the coordinates of all the vertices.

_____

_____

_____

Reflect

(3,9) and (3,5) are two points on the same straight line.
Is the line horizontal or vertical? Explain your answer.

_____

_____

_____

Reasoning on a grid

1 Amelia is drawing a rectangle.

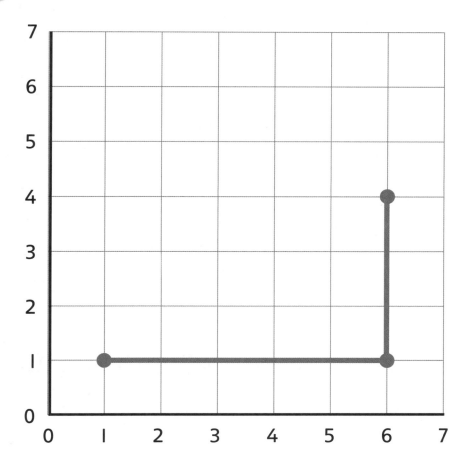

Complete the rectangle and write the coordinates of all four vertices.

 ([ ] , [ ]).

 ([ ] , [ ]).

 ([ ] , [ ]).

 ([ ] , [ ]).

2 Mo is drawing a square on the grid with sides 4 units in length. He has already plotted a point for the bottom left corner of the square.

a) Can you work out the coordinates of the other corners of the square without drawing it? They are:

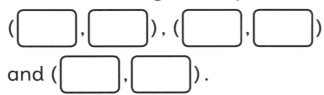 ,

and (⬚ , ⬚) .

b) Draw the square and check your answers.

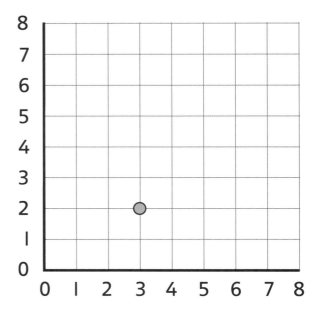

3 Carrie draws three more rectangles exactly the same size as this one. Every rectangle has a corner at (4,4). Draw what the three other rectangles could be.

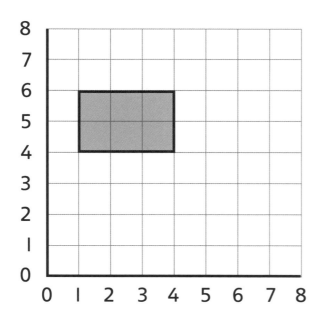

4 This is part of a shape.

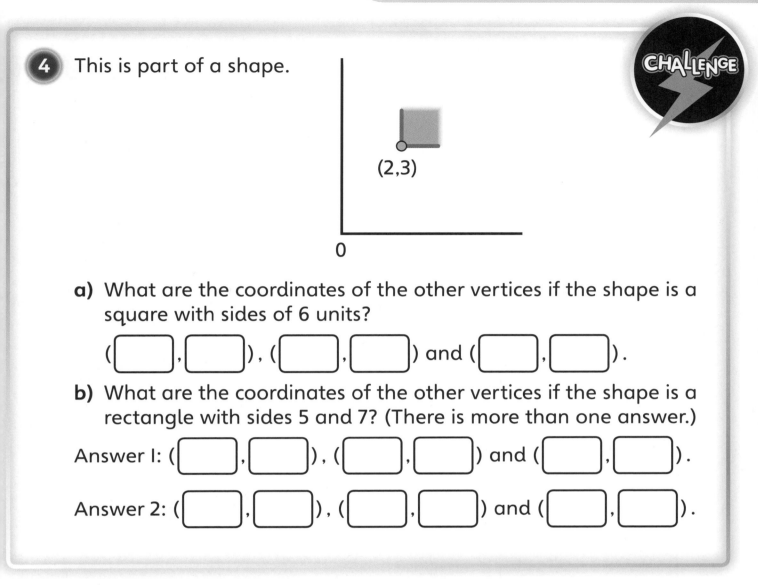

(2,3)

0

CHALLENGE

a) What are the coordinates of the other vertices if the shape is a square with sides of 6 units?

(⬜ , ⬜) , (⬜ , ⬜) and (⬜ , ⬜) .

b) What are the coordinates of the other vertices if the shape is a rectangle with sides 5 and 7? (There is more than one answer.)

Answer 1: (⬜ , ⬜) , (⬜ , ⬜) and (⬜ , ⬜) .

Answer 2: (⬜ , ⬜) , (⬜ , ⬜) and (⬜ , ⬜) .

Reflect

Apart from coordinates, what other mathematical knowledge did you use in this lesson? How did you use this knowledge to answer questions on coordinates?

Moving on a grid

1 On this chart, the instruction 1 right, 1 down will move the boat to the island.

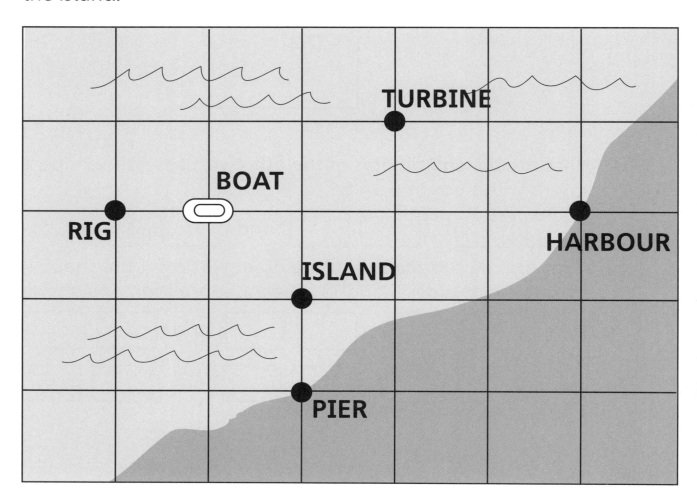

Where would these instructions take the boat? Start back at the same place each time.

a) 1 right, 2 down _____

b) 2 right, 1 up _____

c) 1 left _____

d) 4 right _____

2 A robot starts at (5,5) and moves from point to point around the grid:

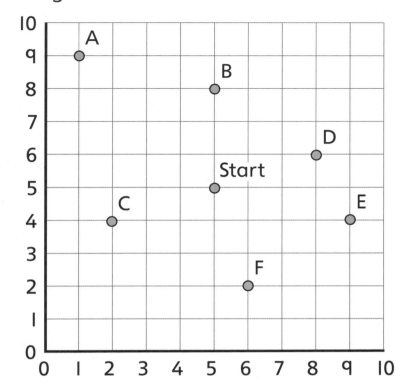

3 right, I up

7 left, 3 up

I right, 5 down

3 right, 4 up

I right, 6 down

3 right, 2 up

What order does the robot visit the points in?

Start → D → _____ → _____ → _____ → _____ → _____

3 Starting at (2,2), the instruction 2 right, I up takes you to (4,3).

Always starting from (2,2), where would these instructions take you?

a) 2 right, I down (⬜ , ⬜)

b) I left, I up (⬜ , ⬜)

c) 2 left, 2 down (⬜ , ⬜)

d) 0 right, 2 up (⬜ , ⬜)

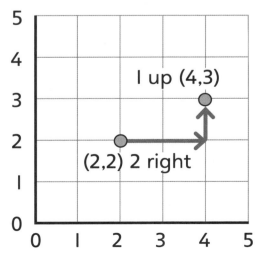

139

4 **a)** You start at the point (100,100). Where would the move

26 left, 26 up take you?   (⬚ , ⬚)

b) You make the move (28 right, 28 down) and arrive

at (100,100). Where did you start?   (⬚ , ⬚)

5 The rectangle is shifted 6 right and 5 up. What are the coordinates of the corners of the rectangle in its new position?

CHALLENGE

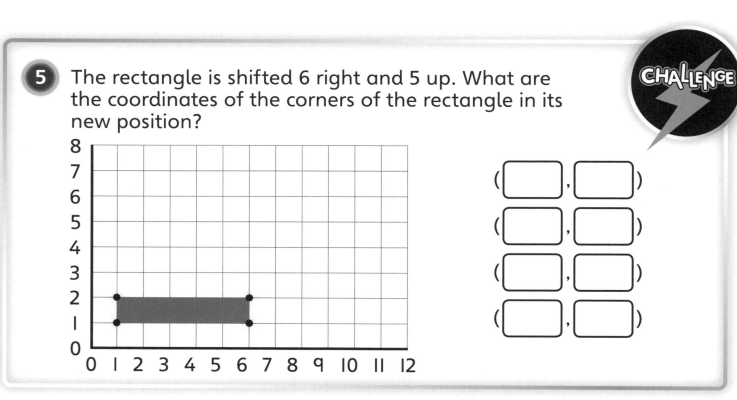

(⬚ , ⬚)

(⬚ , ⬚)

(⬚ , ⬚)

(⬚ , ⬚)

Reflect

The coordinates at the start and end of a move can tell you whether you moved up or down, and left or right.

Do you agree? Explain your answer.

_____

_____

Describing a movement on a grid

1 This map shows the rows of bookshelves in a library.

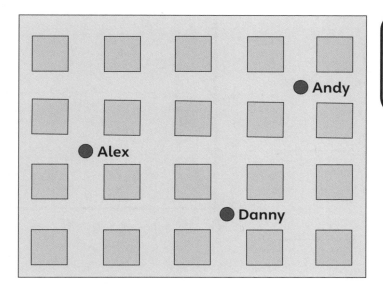

I am going to meet Danny. I will count shelves; I need to go 2 right and 1 down.

Alex

Describe these journeys.

a) Andy goes to meet Danny.

Andy goes ☐ left, ☐ down

b) Danny goes to meet Alex.

Danny goes ☐ _____ , ☐ _____

c) Danny goes to meet Andy.

Andy goes _____ , _____

d) Andy goes to meet Alex.

Andy goes _____

2 To go from A to B, move **I right, 3 up** or **3 up, I right**.

Describe these journeys:

a) B to A

[ ]——— , [ ]———

b) B to C

[ ]——— , [ ]———

c) E to D

————————— , —————————

d) D to E

————————— , —————————

e) D to C

—————————————————

f) A to D

—————————————————

3 First I moved 3 right and 2 up;
then I moved I left and I up.

Reena

Describe Reena's complete journey.

Reena moved _____

142

4 This chess piece can move to any of the squares marked with a circle.

How would you describe each of these moves?

_____

_____

_____

_____

_____

_____

_____

CHALLENGE

Reflect

You know the numbers that describe a movement (for example, 5 left, 2 up).

How would you describe the opposite movement that would take you back to your starting position?

_____

_____

_____

→ Textbook 4C p196

End of unit check

My journal

1 Start at (5,5). Choose two cards, and make the moves shown on the cards, one after the other.

Example: Cards A and F will take you from (5,5) to (9,6).

A	5 left, 10 up

D	10 right, 5 down

B	9 left, 9 up

E	14 left, 4 up

C	2 left, 3 up

F	9 right, 9 down

Which pair of cards will take you from (5,5) to (10,10)?
Explain your answer.

Cards _____ and _____ will take you from (5,5) to (10,10) because

_____

_____

_____

2 Jamir and Kim are playing a game of 4-in-a-line.

- The first player to get four of their counters in any straight line wins the game.

- Jamir has just put a counter in position (5,3).

It is Kim's turn to place a black counter. What position should she put it in to win the game?

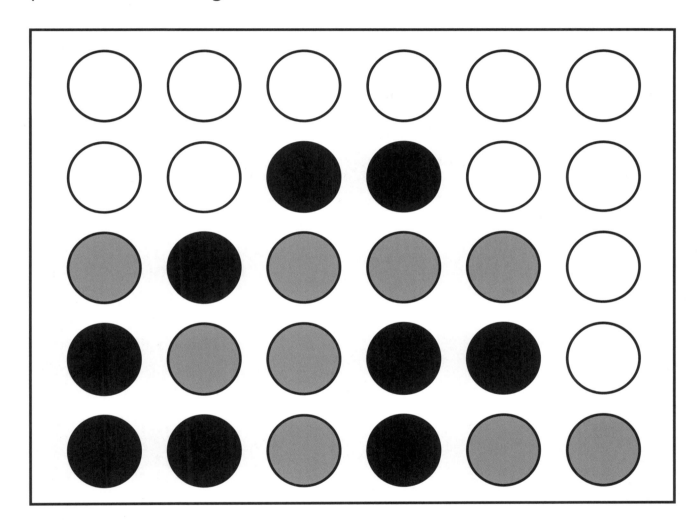

Power play

Coordinate battleships is a game for two players.

- Agree patterns of dots to represent ships.

- Mark your ships on your grid – do not let your partner see where you put them! Your ships must not touch each other.

- Take turns to pick coordinates. Tell your partner whether their shot was a hit or a miss.

- Sink all your partner's ships to win.

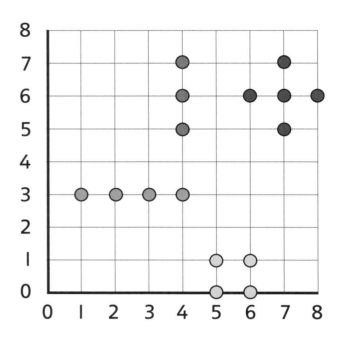

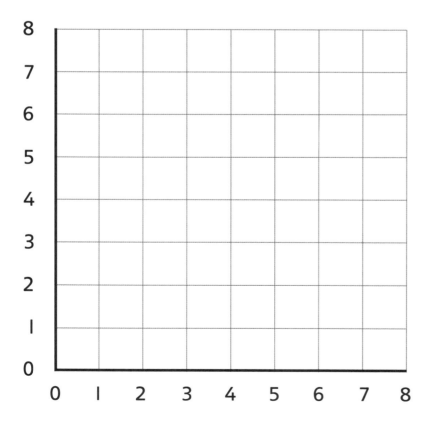

Allow each player to change the shape of one ship. The changed ship must have the same number of dots.

My power points

Colour the ☆ next to the topics you have done.

Colour the ☺ when you feel confident about the topic.

Unit 11
I can ...

☆ ☺ Add two decimals to make a whole

☆ ☺ Write numbers with up to 2 decimal places

☆ ☺ Compare and order decimals

☆ ☺ Round decimals to the nearest whole number

☆ ☺ Write decimal equivalents for $\frac{1}{2}$, $\frac{1}{4}$ and $\frac{3}{4}$

☆ ☺ Convert between different units of measure

Unit 12
I can ...

☆ ☺ Write money in pounds and pence, using a decimal point

☆ ☺ Order, add and subtract amounts of money

☆ ☺ Round money to the nearest 10p or £1

☆ ☺ Find change

☆ ☺ Solve simple word problems involving money

Unit 13
I can ...

☆ ☺ Convert between units of time

☆ ☺ Write times in different ways

☆ ☺ Compare times by converting units

☆ ☺ Solve problems about units of time

Unit 14

I can …

☆ ☺ Present data in pictograms, bar charts and tables

☆ ☺ Interpret line graphs

☆ ☺ Solve problems based on data

Unit 15

I can …

☆ ☺ Recognise obtuse, acute and right angles

☆ ☺ Identify regular and irregular shapes

☆ ☺ Name and describe quadrilaterals and triangles

☆ ☺ Identify lines of symmetry in shapes and patterns

Unit 16

I can …

☆ ☺ Use numbers to say where things are on a grid

☆ ☺ Plot points on a grid

☆ ☺ Use my knowledge of shapes to complete diagrams

☆ ☺ Describe movements on a grid

Keep up the good work!

Notes

Notes

Squared paper

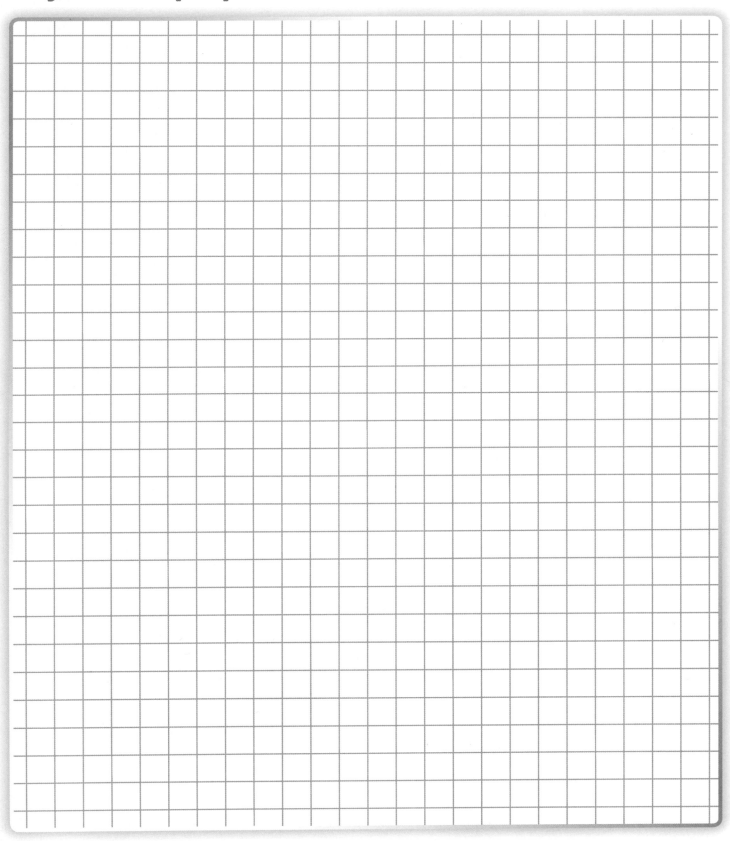

Squared paper

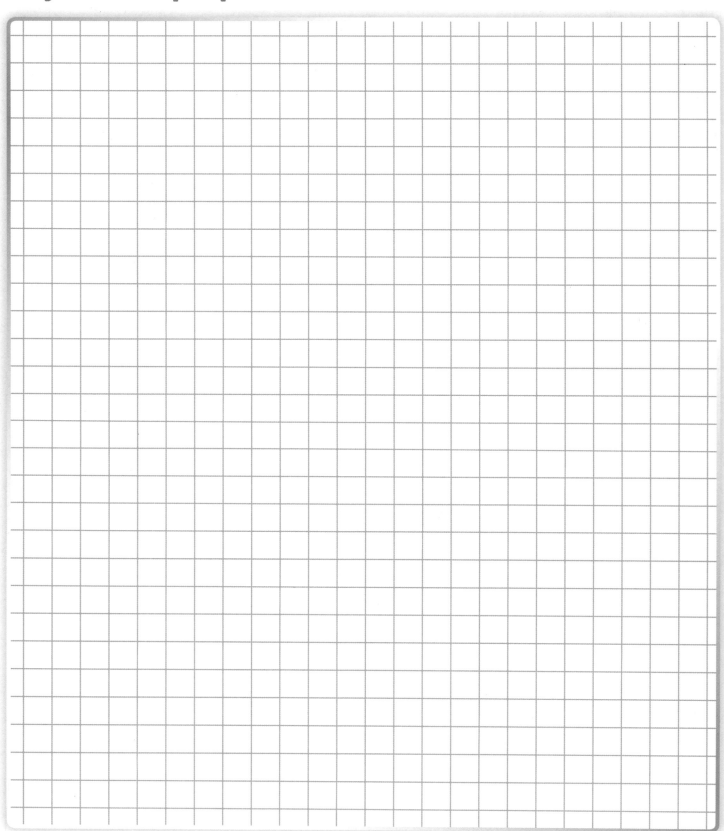